MAUN
A Meeting with Silence

Dr Nirmala Sewani
with
Annie Miller

HAY HOUSE INDIA
New Delhi • London • Sydney
Carlsbad, California • New York City

Hay House Publishers (India) Pvt Ltd
Muskaan Complex, Plot No. 3, B-2, Vasant Kunj, New Delhi – 110070, India

Hay House LLC, P.O. Box 5100, Carlsbad, CA 92018-5100, USA
Hay House UK Ltd, The Sixth Floor, Watson House, 54 Baker Street, London W1U 7BU, UK
Hay House Australia Publishing Pty Ltd, 18/36 Ralph St., Alexandria NSW 2015, Australia

Email: contact@hayhouse.co.in
Website: www.hayhouse.co.in

Copyright © Annie Miller 2024

The views and opinions expressed in this book are the author's own and the facts are as reported by her. They have been verified to the extent possible, and the publishers are not in any way liable for the same.

All rights reserved. No part of this publication may be reproduced, by any mechanical, photographic, or electronic process, or in the form of a phonographic recording, nor may it be stored in a retrieval system, transmitted, or otherwise be copied for public or private use – other than for 'fair use' as brief quotations embodied in articles and reviews – witout prior written permission of the publisher.

The author of this book does not dispense medical advice or prescribe the use of any technique as a form of treatment for physical, emotional, or medical problems without the advice of a physician, either directly or indirectly. The intent of the author is only to offer information of a general nature to help you in your quest for emotional, physical, and spiritual well-being. In the event you use any of the information in this book for yourself, the author and the publisher assume no responsibility for your actions.

First published by Hay House India, 2024

ISBN 978-81-19554-27-0
ISBN 978-81-19554-68-3 (ebook)

Maun: A Meeting with Silence takes one on a personal workshop of the mind and intelligence. It is a powerful journey of wordlessness and subtle experiences, amid the chaos of the external. This book offers a refreshing canvas of the feminine mind and her discovery of truth.

—**Gulab Kothari**
Writer, author, and editor-in-chief, *Rajasthan Patrika*

Maun is an empowering celebration of the human spirit. Each chapter unfolds like a new adventure, revealing layers of resilience, intuition, and self-discovery. It's an exploration of the connection between silence and thought, inviting readers to ponder life's mysteries.

The book is an imaginatively written testament to the strength of character, offering a unique perspective on the challenges and triumphs of an unconventional life. Whether you seek inspiration or a captivating story, this memoir is a compelling read that leaves an impression, nevertheless.

—**Divya Kumar Jain**
Managing Director, Jai Hind Group

Maun skilfully intertwines genres, seamlessly blending the art of storytelling and memoir. The intriguing philosophical and metaphysical elements are truly engaging and lure the reader into a deeper understanding of the world through the lens of Dr Nirmala Sewani.

—**Vinod Bhardwaj**
Writer, journalist, author, and feature editor, *Dainik Bhaskar*

Maun is a brilliantly engaging and thought-provoking narrative with a deep insight into the metaphysical world. This remarkable memoir beautifully captures a journey of resilience and courage of the human heart.

—**Meenakshi Gupta**
Ex-consultant and principal, G. D. Goenka Public Schools

Maun: A Meeting with Silence is a beautiful depiction of the astonishing journey of an ordinary woman's transcendence into the extraordinary. It is a book with an immense heart. An inspiring, thought-provoking read recommended for the young and old alike.

—**Vidya Jain**
Writer, author, director, Centre for Gandhian Studies, University of Rajasthan, and secretary general, Asia Pacific Peace Research Association (APPRA)

Maun is an adventurous journey, like surfing the waves of an ocean. It prepares one for the universal experiences of vulnerability, uncertainty, complexity, and adversity in life. This memoir is a generous synthesis of Nirmala's nascent innocence and understanding of her beatific self. Seriously engrossing and an unputdownable book that explores the interconnectedness of the universe, consciousness, and super-consciousness.

—**Aparna Sahay**
Ex-chairperson, Vishaka, member secretary, Rajasthan State Commission for Women, and chairperson, Manthan and SARA, Jaipur

In *Maun*, the author picturesquely illustrates a resilient woman's exploration into the necessity of stillness in a turbulent world. This beautifully textured book is a worthwhile read and a meditation on the divine significance of silence.

—**Dr S. P. S. Bakshi**
CMD, Bakson Group, and former president, Central Council of Homoeopathy, India

Contents

Author's Note	7
Preface	9
A Reminiscence	13

Chapter 1
Magnolia Walls — 15

Chapter 2
Light Footed Pearls — 21

Chapter 3
Dear Ganesh — 35

Chapter 4
Engraved in Gold — 45

Chapter 5
The Axis of Effort — 51

Chapter 6
Nine Nights — 59

Chapter 7
Echoes without a Whisper — 73

Chapter 8
Impressions — 79

Chapter 9
Back to the Beginning — 87

Chapter 10
Jigsaw Puzzles — 95

Chapter 11
Arrows in Flight — 107

Contents

Chapter 12 A Turtle Retreats	117
Chapter 13 The Quintessence of Generosity	131
Chapter 14 Standing in the Doorway	141
Chapter 15 The Story of a Star	149
Chapter 16 Through the Open Door	165
Chapter 17 A Blank Unknown	179
Chapter 18 A Set of Brass Scales	191
Chapter 19 The Hidden Womb	205
Chapter 20 The Dividing Line	215
Chapter 21 Panigraha	227
Chapter 22 A Carefree Odhni	239
Chapter 23 An Honourable Passing	255
Author's Afternote	263
Acknowledgements	265
About Nirmala Sewani	267
About Annie Miller	268
Glossary	269

Author's Note

One idle conversation and hundreds of questions later, I absorbed Nirmala's story spoken in ceremonial Hindi, while also recording and taking notes religiously, wherever I was. As I deconstructed several words to render legitimate sense in the translation, Nirmala was mostly patient though occasionally, a tone of exasperation cut through her calming voice. There are many phrases used as original for Hindi speakers—with contextual interpretations applied alongside in English. Lastly, although I interviewed mentors, family, and friends to understand different opinions, for most of the work, I stuck to Nirmala's memories and perspectives. This is her story, her poetry, and her voice.

—Annie Miller

Preface

'One world for us all,
Yet each one's world is different.'

Personally, these lines emphasise a humbling truth, not because I have read them somewhere, but because we breathe and live this phenomenon.

Imagine millions of tiny globules or dot-like sensations darting in different directions, often crossing each other, or even colliding if the attraction is powerful. This comprises the world of thought. Our thoughts are like waves on the surface of a sea—interconnected, never ceasing, and constantly flowing in a unique path. And these thoughts generate sensations, pulsations, or vibrations.

Now imagine millions of people with a billion more thoughts, thriving in their own mental worlds and vibrating at different frequencies. Each person passionately embraces the potential of one's individual idea and acts accordingly. Yet, all humans coexist in the same world that we collectively share, love, and fight for. Thus, I reiterate, 'One world for us all . . . yet each one's world is different.'

I have grown within this vast mental realm, a world of thoughts and attractions. Over decades of active engagement, I have constantly tuned into numerous thought frequencies—some gentle, others loud; some vague, others clear; some peaceful, others intense, and some occasionally disconcerting.

It is similar to tuning into the frequencies of various radio stations. Each person thinks uniquely, comprehends differently, communicates, behaves or performs distinctly and thus resides in one's personal, exclusive mental world. And because every thought emits its distinct vibrational force, it attracts a corresponding resonance, much like the pull of a magnet. These vibrations, whether from thoughts or magnets, are imperceptible to our senses—we cannot touch, smell, taste, see, or hear them, yet they exist and exert their influence. A small magnet draws a small nail, while a larger magnet compels a more substantial piece of iron towards it. Likewise, influential individuals continually impact, guide or control developing minds.

Often, while interacting, I observe how an individual's thoughts, emotions, and mental state influence one's voice, an extraordinary yet often overlooked phenomenon. Just as thoughts are distinctive to each person, so is every voice unique. This is because thoughts precede words. You may wonder how. Each thought generates a vibration through which words travel. A sad thought results in a melancholic voice, an angry thought produces a resentful tone, while an enthusiastic thought infuses the same voice with joy. So, in essence, I contemplate the vibrations in a voice.

The word *'maun'* broadly interprets as the absence of spoken words. As a discipline, it strictly involves not using one's vocal cords, which I diligently practised. Not one word escaped my lips, yet my thoughts raced faster than the sprints of Usain Bolt. The speed shocked me. I struggled with an onslaught of random pictures, words, ideas, reflections, and opinions, all bursting into my 'silent' space. Intensely personal, provocative, indulgent, sensory, soothing, illuminating, awkward, and uncomfortable thoughts flooded my mind. I could not deny, escape, or kill this world within me, until finally, a steadiness emerged. And I wondered . . . maun or an intimate meeting with thought?

Just as vast expanses of water, airwaves, sound waves, light waves, electric waves, heat waves and cold waves envelop us, so do thought waves surround us constantly—a tremendous vibration with the power to create, influence, love, hate, destroy, and control, all within the realm of our ever-present emotional mind.

As a child, I could not comprehend or recognise my ability to predict or access the subconscious but gradually, the practice of maun, compelled a growing distance between random thought, focused thought, and no-thought. I grew wary of mundane thoughts. A profound clarity trickled in, and now, while observing, contemplating, and reflecting in silence, I witness myself as a tiny yet intrinsic part of nature's intelligence. I acknowledge this interdependence. There is so much beauty in flowing with life, not against it.

In my silences, I have witnessed the individual mind and its connection to the source—an invisible cosmic mind filled with countless thought vibrations constantly permeating the surrounding atmosphere. Consciously and subconsciously, humans absorb these thoughts with each passing breath. It is food you could say: nourishment from thoughts imbued with care, love, simplicity, and generosity to those thoughts laden with toxicity, anger, jealousy, aggression, lust, and control. In reality, we do not have a choice.

Yet, at life's crossroads, I choose to respond with generosity because it has the beautiful knack of multiplying a hundredfold. Generosity keeps depravity at bay. It nudges me gently towards an innocence and a sweet simplicity I knew as a child. When you read and contemplate this work, be generous. Hold an age-old precept in your mind and heart:

'What is simple . . . is natural.
Innate simplicity is rare knowledge in itself.'

I wish this knowledge for you.

—**Dr Nirmala Sewani**

A Reminiscence

Maa's passing. A defining moment. Like a fruit falling off a tree. Abandoned from its roots. Her blessing . . . a renewed wish. To unlearn, to learn again.

Rummaging through society until then, I made a somewhat impressionable mark. Convinced of life's lasting impermanence, I found a taint, a smear, a wasting in it all. I still do. Yet, even as a wretched brevity etches my heart, I know Maa nurtured my silences, enabling deep spaces to encircle my consciousness. I feel liberated. It is like a two-way door. A release and an expansion to something whispering all along. Persistent. Enduring. Constantly growing.

> 'A magnificence.
> A sacred space.
> A reverberating echo.
> An inspiration.
> And a wish to share.'

— **Dr Nirmala Sewani**

1
Magnolia Walls

 It was well past midnight when Maa screamed my name so loud it woke the neighbours to the far left and right, illuminating a dark night just like the carnival. Ours was the third house to the right on a crowded street in Jyoti Nagar. Two elderly men unlatched our little iron gate and called out to mother.

With a shocked expression, pale skin, and a feverish tone, Maa pointed to the temple room. 'It's Baby. She's wide-eyed and blank. My girl, Baby is not moving at all, and I think she is dead in there,' Maa stumbled through her words.

Sharp seven on a bright and crisp winter morning in 1977, dressed in a bright yellow and gold bordered *paushak*, the twelve-year-old 'Baby'—as they nicknamed me—walked with a flair and a twirl to the temple of our family home. I rearranged my olive green *odhni* to cover my head, while kneeling on a vermillion red, tightly filled pudgy square floor cushion. I took a small matchbox in my left hand and struck a flame, carefully lighting a *ghee diya* my mother prepared every morning. I watched the flame grow to a steady height and smiled, acknowledging all the invisible jobs my Maa completed before our day began.

Joining both my palms together in *namaskar*, I bowed, first to all the ancestral idols displayed in sculpted poses on the two-tiered shelves and then upward to the walls adorned with female and male deities in thin, gold-bordered picture frames. I gazed long enough at these heirlooms passed down generations and found relief in the fresh marigold flower garlands placed on the old photos because they served as a welcome reminder of a new day and a new moment.

A dedicated prayer room, a chosen corner of the house, or a shelf reserved for pictures, idols, and objects of veneration is a vital component for faith-driven masses across the world. Our home in Jyoti Nagar, in the old city of Jaipur, Rajasthan, imbibed the ethnic concepts of a classic Sindhi community uprooted from the Sindh region after the extremity of partition. I was born into this spirited group of people whose beliefs, hope, and trust in a better future never subsided, rather it became their anchor.

Ancestral customs, ceremonies, and historical cultural conventions connected our people in the most heart-warming way, helping to mend and heal a broken community cruelly divided by political upheaval just a few decades ago. Each morning, my grandmother, father, mother, aunts, and uncles walked in and out of our small temple before embarking on a new day. This was a tiny space filled with expectations, anticipations, anxieties, hope, reverence, and a daily dose of gratitude.

Personally, I am in awe of colour. Just as I was as 'Baby' at twelve. Before I opened my eyes in the morning, I felt as if I was stepping into a distinct colour zone. Often it was the same hue for a few days, or just a different tone. It enveloped me in its warmth and coolness. At times, I chose an outfit in a similar colour as I did on that day too. On entering our temple, I deliberately looked at all the garishly clothed idols, different shades of flowers, and the contrasting walls around me.

I drew in a deep, slow breath, no rush, for this was my favourite place to be. As I inhaled and exhaled leisurely, a blend of scents caressed my senses. The fragrance of fresh *champa* flowers on the vine just outside the open wooden-framed window along with the swirling smoke from the *mogra*-scented incense wafted through my nose, enveloping me in a comforting embrace. Gazing at the four magnolia walls of the room, I wondered how far smoke travelled, as my eyes followed its trails from the tip of an incense stick rising upwards in circles to the ceiling.

After a while, the wandering eye finally settled on a low shelf in front of me. I was captivated by what lay there: a unique idol, half human and half elephant. Its form had a soft, relaxed posture with smooth rounded knees, a protruding belly, a large pliable trunk, and an unusual anatomy distinctly separate from the humans I saw every day. It brought a smile to my face, and it still does. I thought this entity, Ganesh, must have had a delicious breakfast because it appeared so content. In its presence, I felt safe, relaxed and comfortable. I wondered why. I still do.

Sitting comfortably in the lotus position, my attention turned to another marble idol: Maa Lakshmi, a feminine deity standing in the centre of a hundred-petalled pink lotus flower. I examined her feet delicately placed in the middle of the yellow stigma. The detail fascinated me, and I wondered how it was possible for an adult woman to stand in the centre of a flower without crushing it. I looked at her body curiously and saw she had four slender arms with four hands holding different objects. A pile of thoughts and questions bounced in my head as I sat there, pondering for a long while.

At some point, as I shifted my focus back to the intriguing image of Ganesh, my eyelids drifted into a soft, almost sublime state. External sounds faded into the background, and the vividly hand-painted marble statue of Ganesh became sharper in my mind's eye. I took time to look at every aspect of this creature; the large trunk of an elephant lifted casually as if inhaling the scents from the incense, two enormous ears, welcoming eyes that seemed tiny, curious, and innocent between the sizeable ears and trunk, a distinct navel on a bare belly, and two small sized beautifully chiselled human feet peeking from under the crossed legs.

Oblivious to the physical, tangible world, I felt as though I was floating in a visually dark space, much like a moonless dark night. My core resonated with a steady, hum akin to a resounding heartbeat. I do not have adequate words to articulate that feeling. Yes, it was a silence, yet it reverberated like a deep sound from the centre of a djembe drum, and I receded into its epicentre.

Meanwhile, Maa spent the day attending to her mother-in-law and my five siblings. Her days were chaotic, as she took care of all the needs and wants of our home, like most mothers do. That week, my father was away on a business trip in Maharashtra, the west of India.

As she went about her day, Maa passed the prayer room each time she walked from the corridor to the kitchen, glancing at me sitting there motionless. Relieved to know that one of her six children was sitting quietly, she proceeded to her next task. After preparing dinner, and catering to everyone, Maa returned to the prayer room and gently remarked, 'Baby, you're late for your dinner. Your sisters are all off to bed.'

When I did not respond, she walked past me to check on my brother in the other room, thinking she would be back soon. However, she fell asleep while lying in bed with him.

Sometime past midnight, Maa woke up and walked to the kitchen for a drink of water. She noticed me sitting in the prayer room, just as she had left me hours ago. Maa hurried back to the kitchen returning with a tall glass of saffron milk. Assuming I had fallen asleep, she tried to wake me.

I gazed at her, lost and distant, with wide, unblinking eyes. Maa stared at my unresponsive face, yelled while shaking my shoulders, and panicked, thinking I might have died. She rushed to the front porch, shouting for our neighbour across the street. Her screams woke my sisters, and the lights in the next ten houses came on. In no time, all the elders from the street had gathered on our front porch.

Distracted by the commotion, I returned to my twelve-year-old body, trudged out to the crowd, and tugged at my bewildered Maa. I announced that it was late, I was going to bed, and they should all keep the noise down.

Maa's baffled expressions remain a treasured memory for all of us. This is the one event that lights up our dining table every time we remember it. My second youngest sister, Madhu, often says she never heard Maa scream like she did that night. Sometimes, speaking of this incident brings tears to our eyes, as it reminds my four sisters, brother Shankar, and me of the presence we miss so dearly. Maa held our family together with grace and a quiet resilience I find hard to emulate.

This was my first encounter with the sounds of silence. I sat motionless in a small room for over seventeen hours, experiencing something my adolescent mind did not need to construct in words. After all these years, I still struggle to find an expression or one fitting word for the finer, intangible quality of those hours.

Nevertheless, something shifted during those hours; a strange solidity entered my mind. The constant stream of questions became more defined, more intense, and more urgent. Where did I journey to in that weightless silence? Why didn't I experience the biological pangs of hunger for such an extended period? Why did I lose the sense of time? What were those sounds I heard? The questions were endless, annoying, and unrelenting. I moved about conscious of a clear split within myself, much like a turtle with its outer shield and the secretive interior it continuously retreats into.

To express those delicate nuances one encounters in silence, I often write in Urdu, a language that carries the sounds of a graceful symphony and words that expand in perfect ripples.

So often.
I say to you,
I am lonely
without you since.
I am in love with you,
are you not in love with me?
You fill me up with dreams,
you give me your very life.
Whenever I die within myself,
you appear,
nourishing me with life again.
Each moment I melt into you,
you meet me,
and I blossom.

2
Light Footed Pearls

I gradually discovered I may know or understand something in a broader frame only after walking a thousand miles with it. It often requires persistent engagement—chewing, gnawing, swallowing, and crossing many more hurdles before a word, concept, symbol, mantra, or idea transforms into an inescapable reality. It melts into me. This phase continues until I uncover the inherent paradox and embark on yet another cycle of expansion.

Personally, this journey towards a better understanding is akin to crossing a rickety, irreverent suspension bridge, hanging precariously over turbulent waters. And when I make my way to the other side, I just might discover what lies there. Over the years, I have repeatedly trudged over a particular bridge, which is, crossing between the spoken word on one side to silence on the other.

This rarely travelled journey serves as a continual reminder of a common truth. The word in its prime intention and phonetics manifests beyond the dimensions of this planet. It is the most effective gift for external expression and a privileged medium of gathering, communicating, and evolving for the human species. Yet silence is a force subtler, lighter, and far more expansive than the reaches of sound. A subtlety devoid of the weight or the mass of a word.

In silence, I travel vast spaces I cannot visualise during conversation. My body, senses, vision, and mind ride high waves as stillness unfolds. I cross the threshold to clarity in thought, ideas, and feelings. Then, the words I speak carry the courage I gather deliberately in such phases of silence.

I remember the sheer joy of crossing this bridge spontaneously as a young girl. Silence allowed me to ask simple, straightforward questions, much like most children do. It begins as a natural occurrence with all young individuals until the environment corrupts the mind with a label, an attachment, or a division. A girl or a boy, right or wrong, quiet or loud, well-behaved or disobedient, true or false, left or right, and so on.

I repeatedly asked myself the simplest questions. Who created the trees, the thousands of varieties of flowers, and all these beautiful, vibrant colours I love? Who crafted fish with their precise, symmetrical designs, and who patterned the meandering rivers? I often wondered if I could ever meet the painter, assuming there was one, and if there was that one, then who?

I observed how people in my surroundings interfered with nature, cut down trees, destroyed green stretches, polluted rivers, mistreated animals, and harmed fellow humans, caring little for anything beyond themselves. I watched adults shouting in anger, speaking without reason, and treating one another differently. On my way to school, I counted all the children not wearing school uniforms and wondered why. People prayed in temples but littered the path outside. What was the problem or the need?

I constantly felt an immense sadness. It was as if I was surfing a succession of waves, both large and small, rising and ebbing as days turned into nights; waves of anger, despair, frustration, confusion, and helplessness. At that age, I did not understand these feelings or know as many words to express emotions.

I noticed how one person followed another. Someone did it, so another did the same. I did what I did because I watched others do it. We were all following, with no one stepping out of line. I made observations at school too. On certain days, when students did not conform, the teacher dragged them back into the line. It confused me. Who established the rules, and why? What was wrong with walking a little apart, slightly separated from the crowds?

I absorbed questions through the pores of my skin, storing them somewhere beneath the surface. When I remained silent for long stretches, I carried this heavy wretchedness with me but somehow emerged lighter and clearer on the other side. I did not find answers immediately. No, not at all. Yet, each time, I felt a little steadier which enabled me to think, act, and respond differently. I now moved from one day to the next, holding on to how I felt rather than how the other expected me to think or act.

In time, however, a filtered thought entered my mind—a sense of knowing and a 'principle.' I chose learning and realised that those who follow blindly live in ignorance. On the other hand, knowledge is a gift for those who care to lead their feet onto bridges, to perhaps taste the uniqueness of life that awaits one far beyond the countless fears instilled in us.

And yes, when these light-footed pearls arrive, listen well. Hold them gently in secret caves. Contemplate them in the simplicity of silence and do not force the complexity of a hypothesis and dilute them. Let them float softly until they mingle in your bones. Assimilate them until they speak through you, walk with you and dream in you.

A couple of months after that startling experience in the prayer room, one evening, I casually read my horoscope in a book called *Star Scope*, written by Bejan Daruwala. It had a list of lucky days based on the zodiac, with Thursday being the favourable day for Pisces which is my sign. I thought it was a good day to discipline my mind and decided to observe a fast (customary religious abstinence from food).

This act was not unusual, as fasting once a week to please deities is a common practice in most of Southeast Asia. It is a ritual so ingrained in daily life that it often goes unnoticed for what it is—a simple yet profound exercise for one to gather energy at an inner focal point, realign, nurture and restore balance in the mind, body and being.

Every Thursday, Maa cooked my favourite meal, which I ate once a day, usually around 4 p.m. One week, on an exceptionally warm Thursday during the high summer months of Jaipur, I refused to eat because I disliked everything I saw on the plate of food Maa had served.

My poor mother. I pushed the plate away in a huff, while she tried to coax the stubborn twelve-year-old me into eating. Angry and frustrated, I ignored her, choosing to remain silent. I stood by the kitchen door. Maa walked dangerously close to me and stared into my face while placing her hands on her hips. 'Baby, is this some new kind of introspection that refuses me the courtesy of an answer? Why are you so stubborn?' She then looked up to the skies, saying, 'Why do I have a child who enjoys annoying her parents so much?'

It is true; I was stubborn to the bones, and like any girl my age, I hated being told off, so I decided not to speak from that moment onwards right up to the time my fast ended and even longer. In fact, I kept quiet for a long stretch of thirty-five hours. Not one word! My first walk into the world of 'keeping quiet.'

A week later, on Tuesday, I strolled into the kitchen, declaring I would not utter a word on the days I fasted. You had to be there to see the exasperated expression on my mother's face. Not one spoken word, but she gave me a long look that said it all. As usual, she looked up at the heavens again and started chanting to all her gods for mercy. Soon enough, it was Thursday again, and I remained silent from the break of dawn until I headed to school the following morning at half past eight.

I became the talk of the town. The doors to our home were always open. Aunt Shakuntala came to sympathise with my Maa for having a weird daughter. Then, driven by curiosity, she returned to spy on me, checking if I was still 'quiet.' Shakuntala worked at the Vidyut Bhavan, just a mile away from our home, and when she couldn't stomach my silence, she told a colleague at work. Soon we had fifteen men and women checking in to see if the information was genuine. One day, Laxmi, a friend of my aunt, tiptoed into the house at lunch and then at 4 p.m. to catch me talking or speaking aloud to myself. All of it amused me.

In the beginning, when I did not talk for extended periods, the words stopped flowing flying out of my mouth but raced through my head, like a Japanese Shinkansen train at its highest speed. My ears absorbed every sound, as if they didn't want to miss the gossip. And then I could not think beyond food. All the things I liked to eat, I could eat or would eat when I broke my fast. Next, I thought of Maa's cooking—what I liked best— and how I would ask her to make all the savoury and sweet dishes she avoided cooking while I fasted.

'I must stop thinking of food,' I thought, but I had little control over my thoughts or my belly. My mind felt like a crowded train station where everything came in hordes, gate-crashing all restricted areas.

Discontent followed in quick succession. The next week, I criticised everything and everyone. My eyes turned microscopic, scrutinising anything I gazed at. All five senses stood on alert; I smelled the food I ate, observed people serving it, saw my sisters casually playing with all my things, heard my little brother making too much noise, noted the staff dodging corners while cleaning, watched my friends having fun, aunts and uncles getting on with their gossip, and eventually, scanned the entire world hovering around me. They closed in, and I watched everything. I didn't just watch and listen; I observed with a keen, judgemental attitude, discovering how strongly I felt and how my opinion as a teenager did not matter in an adult world. Yet, I persevered, pushing myself, probably because I wanted to win that round.

I am too obstinate to give in or give up easily. Though I succeeded in not speaking aloud, there was a war in capital words inside my head. The chatter didn't end there, and soon I was blaming the creator for denying me the calm that goes with silence. Foremost teachers educate young minds to obey, follow, respect, and learn exactly as the older generations did, and in the seventies, they didn't tutor girls in traditional communities to have a mind of their own. I had just discovered a new freedom and questioned everything that was expected of a young person. I could not grasp the confusion within.

This continued for a year until my mind lost all purpose in it. I found a strange indifference to it all—the people, the stories, and the attitudes. I lost interest. For hours on end, I spoke to Ganesh, seeking help. It was the one aspect I did not doubt—my beautiful reference, the image I loved then, and I love now. My best friend and confidante. I spoke of all my questions, observations, judgements, and reservations. Quietly, I revealed all to this invisible image—my resistance, confusion, doubts, vulnerability, desires, wishes, and my dreams.

The distance between the world and me grew ever so slowly. Week after week, I watched it all, like a movie screen. My first steps into scrutiny—without a word. Everyone adulated me. When grown-up people shower praise on young ones for reassurance, it works as a pump, boosting the pressure. It created a strong will within me, and I fasted week after week in complete outer silence.

Within the next year, the anatomy of my youthful body relaxed into a new pattern. The hunger pangs disappeared, and the thought of food became outdated. If that thought arose, there was a counter thought in the mind, examining the turning of each day, 'What is the hurry now? Do I have to fall for habit, or can I wait?' Somewhere inside of me, a tiny tender shoot was growing stronger each week. I was twelve and a half when I re-trained my mind through observation. I began the process of reversal, reflecting on the repetitive turn of a day after a night. The depth of this consistent phenomenon still has an effect on me. It allows me to listen and slow down rather than follow the speed of a sensory thought always pushing to perform, to do, or to react. Gradually, I eliminated the notion that I had to follow. I realised this by scrutinising each rising impression in an individual frame and then sharply nipping at it. I learnt to lead; not to lead the other, but to direct myself independently.

In silence, one's mind slows down to external activity, but thoughts churn a thousand times faster. Stay with it. Watch it till a sort of percolation and filtering begins. A separation enters the mind, a gentle sifting of a thought—from the mundane to the not-so-mundane. Watch some more, and in time, a habit disintegrates.

This pattern continued for the next three years. I skipped school on a Thursday, woke early, and did not talk, eat, or drink any other liquid except one glass of water (carefully calculating the sips to last longer). I slept at nine pm and woke at seven am on Friday, dressed quietly and walked for three and a half miles to Prem Shanti Public School at the edge of Jyoti Nagar. From age twelve to fifteen, I often missed school on Thursdays, attending only if there was a class test, examination, or a practical test in the laboratory. When teachers posed questions, I wrote the answers on a piece of paper. My classmates giggled, teased, tripped and tickled me so I might scream or laugh. I persevered but also gave them a piece of my mind the next day. Gradually, my friends rallied around me, making it easier to maintain my practice.

Often, at night, I lay in bed contemplating a myriad of questions. I thought of the inherent impressions that each baby comes into this world with. How does that happen? Why did I feel compelled to follow my instincts and embrace silence when no one else around me did? What makes one walk a different path without fear? Why are we all so different? How could I access the vibrations in a voice or thought to know a personality or a blueprint?

A decade later, I wrote in my diary, 'All creatures are in constant flow, in a river of movement—a force that carries the animate and the inanimate. This energy travels within our environments, making impressions in the senses, intellect, and the subconscious. The most effective vehicle for travelling impressions is listening, after which comes the spoken word and the written follows, each with the ability to influence, manipulate, and shape oneself and another. Thus, we form habits. We follow.'

For instance, if one comments on another in group A, a conveyance takes place, and the comment travels to a different audience of listeners. The one who comments makes an impression, negative or positive, affecting the person commented upon. Similarly, the body—which is matter—eventually dies but the impressions remain in the subtle bodies—the mind and intellect.

Amidst such observations, solitude and quiet became precious tools, relieving me from the weight of the day, and nudging me lightly into the bliss of a quiet night.

I was eighteen when, my younger sister, Vanita, started observing the Vedic nine-day fasting ritual, eating home-cooked food once a day. Three years younger than me, Vanita is still an ardent follower of the feminine divinity, while I've always silently revered the more elusive myth of Ganesh. Traditionally, the Vedic almanac designates four periods in a year, each lasting nine nights, for worshipping the feminine, of which two are widely celebrated, and the other two discreetly observed by keepers and seekers of the tradition.

In October 1981, I imitated Vanita, observing the fast too but with a slight twist; I decided not to speak for the whole stretch of the nine-day fasting period, announcing my idea just the night before. And when I did, there was a sudden crash in the stillness of the living room. I heard jumbled thoughts scurrying across the centre of the room like scooters at a busy traffic intersection and soon all five of my siblings left the room in a huff.

I rarely changed my mind for anyone, not even my mother, who quietly retreated to the kitchen, and probably started praying to all thirty-three million deities for common sense. Based on my decision to stay silent for the nine day/night period also meant not eating food altogether, because the process involves sounds like crunching, chewing, and smacking of the lips. But my father insisted I drink a glass of milk at dawn and dusk and a glass of water in between. I agreed.

I have never over analysed the many decisions I make. Somehow, the first organic thought is what I stay steady with and that gives me the nerve and endurance to see it through. In fact, if a decision involves too much thought, I have mostly abandoned that idea.

My youngest sister, Seetu, questions my ways. She says I take instant decisions—before the others have even processed the idea. It leaves little space for a collaborated opinion or a collective decision. From the simplest of verdicts in choosing colours and styles of dresses for all my sisters to every other decision that mattered in their lives, I decided, almost too quickly sometimes. And in this instance too, I had made up my mind to stay silent and go without food for the nine-day period. Day one was easy because my mind and tongue were both trained for a twenty-four-hour silent process. My body was geared for fasting too.

On day two, I succeeded with an outwardly silence but my stomach spoke louder by the hour. It was demanding food. The elusive fangs of pride surfaced just behind the craving. I watched myself closely, realising how much the last three years had helped. It enabled me to maintain a short distance between my intention and the emerging thoughts. As the sun went down that evening, I gulped a big tumbler of warm milk and hit my bed.

The next three days were hellish. There was nothing holy or profound about them. I kept myself busy with odd jobs around the house, cleaning, running errands, and meeting people who requested astrological interventions. I communicated with them via a notepad.

In hindsight, at eighteen, I observed a lot more than normal. I watched my mother serve the mother-in-law, the gardener nursing tender flower beds like newborn babies, and my sisters going about their day, oblivious to the war in my head. People walked in and out all day, commenting but not affected whatsoever. Looking, but not watching. Hearing, but not listening. Talking, but not reflecting. This observation changed my attitude towards everything, and I jotted my inferences down. The human mind caught in itself, lives, breathes and thinks with itself as the central focus. It performs externally yet thrives in a thought world. It was an interesting phase. I became even more meticulous in my daily chores. Perfection was the key. I had little or no patience for the lack of discipline, cleanliness, or order.

On day five, I cursed and insulted everything. While my sisters relished delicious treats like fried potatoes, sweet potato salad and *sago dana dahi vada*, I criticised the concept of eating during a fast. I relentlessly judged everyone. My head ran around in circles, not knowing if I was more furious with the world or myself—or both. Who was I competing with, anyway? I observed the see-saw motion of the mind and watched it like the eye of a hawk in mid-air, waiting to pounce on its prey. I watched my pride tumbling, and I watched the arrogance of a competitive mind. I spent hours thinking about what it meant to take responsibility for our actions. If I started something, I had to see it through, never mind if it was right or wrong, good or bad. I came to understand how easily we deflect responsibility in the many layers of blame, self-pity, and expectations. We often attribute the failure of our endeavours to external circumstances, abandoning our once-enthusiastic pursuits.

So, during this process, I began the long and tedious journey of self-scrutiny. I saw the vacillating mind, denied it, worked against it, and exhausted myself with it, until eventually, I accepted what I saw. I wrote all my observations, looking at them over and over again. I was impatiently curious to know more about what was inside of me. Humans follow one another, yet we are all so unique. In silence, I discovered the accumulation of every breath I have taken since birth. The air we breathe, the touch we feel and respond to, the pictures we click with the blink of our eyes, the tastes we discover and the smells we follow. As the years passed, I had little choice but to watch the effect of different environments within myself and others. Because of my ability to access the thought revolving in a vibration, I discovered the difference between assumption and reality, arrogance and humility, generosity and greed, lust and love, and impulses versus endurance. I was beginning to know my mind better.

After recognising within myself, what I observed in others, I finally realised how incomplete I was. For months, every interaction felt personal; like looking into a mirror. When I came across anger, I found anger within me. When I called out the arrogance in others, I felt it surging through me. When I encountered stubborn attitudes, I discovered how obstinate I could be.

It took way more than one nine-day period of maun to realise that I was a wave in the vast ocean of existence. This one wave carried the essence of the entire ocean—love, hate, jealousy, anger, greed, compassion, pride, and a generous heart. I was all of it. I finally surrendered.

The nine-day period also helped me to actively learn mantras and chant them in repetition. This practice made the last two days of fasting almost non-existent as I spent most waking hours repeating chants and later sleeping for the sheer lack of energy. I was stubborn and I still am. It is an exquisite quality once understood—stubbornness carved me; it emboldened me, and it melted me in subtle ways.

On the tenth day, I woke early with a mental list of tasks which I jotted in the now-famous notepad. The Sewani household buzzed with excitement on Ram Navami—the tenth day—a colourful feast for the senses. Fresh marigold flowers adorned every home, girls strutted in their silk dresses and delicate jewellery while the delightful aroma of mouth-watering *halwa poori*, cooked in pure ghee, wafted through the air, into the bedecked streets.

Dressed in a deep red, gold-bordered paushaak, with my long hair braided in fresh mogra flowers, I felt both generous and light. A renewed softness entered my being on the last day.

I led a fire ceremony for our family, chanting mantras with a steadiness that penetrated the core of my stomach. Not one wave in the sea. Imagine that. It felt as if something impossible or unknown suddenly became plausible and known.

This was the beginning of my long journey into the realms of silence. The start of the sprouting of a seed into a delicate, tiny bud. Now, I had nothing but intent, time and patience as companions. After the success of this first venture came forth a fresh wave of determination and an indomitable spirit. I had achieved what I set out to do and with that high, I persevered.

The next nine-day fasting period came in three months—one of the two lesser-known Navratri events, more for seekers or the adept.

Although only a few fasted during this period, the journey began in high spirits with no problems on day one. I chanted mantras, tidied my room and helped around the house. By the end of day two, I found myself just a degree less agitated than the last time. I slept well too feeling confident and determined in my resolve. But that was the end of my bliss. Days four and five were like a trip on the turbulent Irish seas. I felt like a seasick person on a boat that showed no signs of anchoring. I struggled but held myself quietly to the end of nine days, realising that something had shifted since the last time. More questions cascaded my mind, while my senses wandered further, catching distant conversations, sounds, smells and fragrances. I absorbed the slightest movement. I felt it all—the tingling sensations of the tongue without tasting, the heightened sense of touch, the awareness of a drop of water touching the body or the gentle brush of a passing fly.

I often wonder if the journey to self-discovery was any easier for ascetics. I cannot say. What I do know is that I am an integral part of this pulsating world in its entirety—every aspect, every detail, and every colour. I feel the tiniest grain of sand upon it. I am a unique part of every shape created through this phenomenon. Therefore, I sense it all. I am not inclined to walk away from it. I do not need to—there is nowhere to go.

Just one life, and you are one.
With you, I wish
to enclose time in tightly clenched fists.
I wish to fill my voiles
with the blue in the sky.
Just one life, and you are one.
I wish to fly away with you.
I wish to imagine each path as the purpose.
Just one life, and you are one.
I wish to hold your hand through every journey.
In all relationships, in every manner,
I wish to make you mine.
Just one life, and you are one.
With you, I wish to become like you.
The splendour of colours and the glow of lamps,
I wish to see it all through your eyes.
Just one life, and you are one.
I wish to feel each celebration
through your senses.
Just one life, and you are one.

3
Dear Ganesh

By the end of primary school in 1976, I acquired various prefixes to my name—Devi, Maa, Baby Maa, Didi Maa, Bai Sa, Babyji, Nirmalaji, and a strange one—Napoleon gypsy. This one possibly because I wore beautiful flowing skirts and spoke my mind fearlessly like a nomadic, carefree woman. Or perhaps, it could be the historical hearsay about the travellers who predicted Napoleon's defeat at Waterloo.

Anyway, I discovered my intuitive side while speaking words and sentences about everyday situations, such as when one might find the love of her life, or the life expectancy of an ailing parent. Some asked for auspicious dates to begin a business venture, and mothers asked how their children might fare in their examinations or first jobs and so on. Interestingly, most of the information I gave, was correct. In those days, word spread faster than the pigeon that flew in with a note and soon the entire community, neighbours, relatives, family, and their friends came calling in for predictions of all sorts. Our home was more like a busy waiting room, with complimentary tea and biscuits offered all day long.

I vividly recall a summer afternoon, when I entered the house on my way back from school with Vanita. We had just taken our shoes off when my father called me into the living room. Two men sat on the two-seater sofa beside my father's armchair.

'Baby, please help this man,' my father said, gesturing towards one man who greeted me with folded hands.

'How may I help?' I asked quickly, eager to head for a cold shower.

The tall man looked tired and anxious. He said, 'Devi, my son has gone missing without a trace. Please tell me what you can and where I can find him. Is he alive?'

Seated next to my father, I folded my hands and said, 'Namaskar. I do not know how to. Yes, I can read the *Panchangam* (Indian almanac) but do not have any thoughts on 'the lost and found.' I have no access to anything lost, missing, or stolen.'

The man persisted, 'I have searched everywhere, with my son's friends, relatives, and the police, but no one has any clue or information. Please say something that might bring hope, and if it does not come true, I will not bother you over it.'

I did not know if I could help the man, so I closed my eyes. It was a quiet escape. I always feel reassured when I can shift all attention within me. But then, I saw the distraught face of a father and heard his anxious thoughts. Pictures flashed like a disconnected dream. I saw a young boy sitting at a two-gauge railway crossing. I said it aloud, while voicing the thoughts of that young boy too. 'This boy ran away from home because he wants to be an actor.' After a deliberate pause, and another flash in my head, I said, 'And you would not allow him. You told him off for being useless.'

The man, now mumbling, folded his hands and said, 'Yes, yes. I did. That is true. In what direction should I go? There are so many railway lines around the city. Where do I start?'

I opened my eyes and with little thought, said, 'Go to the west. Go before he goes somewhere else.'

In a couple of days, my father informed me that the men had searched far and found the boy sitting on a two-gauge railway crossing, a hundred miles west of old Jaipur. Unsure of his decision, the boy had not left Jaipur yet.

Now, this man had put up a missing person's notice at a newspaper agency and went back there to withdraw the advertisement. He saw a queue of people reporting their loved ones as 'missing'. They were curious to know how he had found his son. He obliged, telling them how grateful he was, praising my psychic abilities and then directing everyone to me.

In the same week, another man came to the house, desperately searching for his missing daughter. I repeated the same words, 'I do not know anything about lost things or people.' But there was no getting away. Reluctantly, I agreed to say something, although I was apprehensive. A few ramblings had manifested as 'correct' predictions, but I feared the day when things would not come true. My young ten-year-old heart knew it did not want anyone calling me a liar. In fact, I did not want any of this and had little understanding of what was happening.

Nonetheless, I couldn't deny what I felt—the subtlest vibrations in the room, thoughts rippling at great speed, jostling with each other for attention and eventually expanding into the atmosphere. With my eyes open, I voiced a series of thoughts aloud. I told the worried father that his daughter had run away from home. I then picked up the daughter's thoughts. 'The girl fears her father. She is going to marry a Muslim boy not far from here, probably in a village close by.'

The shocked man asked, 'But there are many villages near Jaipur. In which direction should I search?'

I was amused and thought to myself, 'I said 'west' the last time, so I think I will say east now.' My words held true once again, and they found the girl in Alwar minutes before she was to marry a Muslim boy. In the early seventies, society considered inter-caste/faith marriages a violation, especially between a Hindu and a Muslim.

In the next two weeks, more people came, searching for our house and the Devi who made accurate predictions. We lived in a small, closely-knit community where food, troubles, judgements, illnesses, worries, gossip, and celebrations were all shared generously. Once, a neighbour's ailing father lost a kidney, and they asked how long he would live. I predicted six months. The wife, who was my mother's friend, returned a few days after six months, with the news. Despite the man's recovery, he suddenly passed away.

Even as a young girl, I said exactly what I picked up from a vibration—nothing more, nothing less. People approached my parents first, who turned no one away. Kind-hearted and generous, Maa and Daddy, welcomed everyone. Our tiny home turned into a busy marketplace, with each one seeking answers, tea, and dinner, in that sequence.

Many came in asking questions about an illness, monetary crisis, career, marriage, and the usual worries. Sometimes I laughed at the questions, but after every prediction, I also promised myself and dear Ganesh never to predict again. This strong faith people have, or entrust in you, can be overwhelming. It puts pressure on performance. Each time someone requested an unknown answer, I obliged and then ran to the temple room.

Sitting cross-legged with folded hands, I whispered to my only love—Ganesh; my most beautiful friend. You know me better than all these people here. Please let these words fall true one last time, or they will call me a liar. You know I do not lie, and I dislike liars. Just this once, please make my words meaningful.

I do not want them to call you a liar too, so I promise never to predict again. This is the last time, Ganeshji. I will never break this promise. Please, my beautiful dearest friend.'

This was a lie. Everything I said came true, and I have not stopped picking up the thoughts behind a voice ever since. All I ever wanted was beautiful, brightly coloured dresses, bags, pretty sandals, movies, and theatre. I loved dressing up, and I still do. I played the sitar for hours and enjoyed performing in school. Yet, I found myself caught in an unusual situation where I came face to face with many challenging predicaments in a day. I observed, contemplated, and experienced their dilemmas somewhere within the subconscious.

I had just turned thirteen when I stumbled upon the book *The Benham Book on Palmistry* (first printed in 1900) in my father's little library. It transported me to another world. A world of hands, palms and lines. Intrigued, I examined lines on every hand, young and old. The more I studied these lines across different palms, the more I marvelled at the intensive research of a man who studied the palms and fingers of musicians and murderers alike. I tried to look for information on the author's life and discovered he developed an interest in palmistry after a chance meeting with an old traveller woman. Benham noted, 'During this time, the word "palmistry" was so buried under public disapproval that a self-respecting person dared not say he was interested in it. But fully persuaded it had a scientific foundation, and I set about to discover it.'

This world, in a palm, fascinated me so much that I dived headlong into Benham's book. I followed every illustrated diagram on patterns, similarities, and differences of lines. I studied the structure of lines in the four fingers, the curve of a thumb, and the shape of a hand; all from Benham's dense manual. These lines spread into a vast map, like following the widening roots of a tree, invisible to the eye. A whole alternative world opened up, and I could not contain my excitement. I dug my eyes into every hand I encountered. Each line felt like an unexplored pathway waiting for the bearer of that hand to tread upon, to discover and to experience.

One summer afternoon, a small group of girls from school got together at our friend Naina's house. We ate a sumptuous lunch of *chana chawal* and *dasheri aam*—the juiciest, sweetest pulp of mango love. After lunch, we sat on her bed, making fun of each other, tying braids in our hair and dancing. I read the lines on their developing hands, practising what I was studying. After a while, they asked me to tell them of their futures. It was all in good humour and we spoke of boyfriends and marriage. Even in my most relaxed times, I spoke what came. I never flinched, never doubted, or retracted from what I said once.

So, when it was Naina's turn, I said, 'Your sister will run away from home soon.' My friends teased me for such an incredulous idea. While making masala tea in the kitchen, Naina mentioned it to her mother, who laughed at the thought and vouched for her other daughter, saying, 'You girls are wicked, but my Gurmeet is an angel who will do nothing of the kind.' We playfully tormented her, asking who she thought was the best among us and why she was calling us names.

'Look at our faces, auntie. Do you see any mischief?' I teased.

The next week, I went to the shops with Maa and bought a pair of sandals with silver straps. Excited to wear them the next day after school, I showered, changed into a beautiful green dress, and headed straight to the shoe rack. My gorgeous new sandals were missing.

I was so angry I brought the house down. Maa finally spoke when I stopped yelling. 'Baby, calm down. Gurmeet came an hour ago. She wore them and left her old slippers here instead. I am sure she will come back soon.'

'How dare she?' I said and headed straight to her house to bring back my lovely pair of silver sandals. When I got there, I saw people pacing up and down and met her anxious mother yelling and wailing. Well, Gurmeet, my friend Naina's older sibling, had run away from home. The mother looked at me furiously, thinking I had a hand in it. Then I saw my father, who immediately jumped towards me, clasped my slender right wrist with his big heavy hand, and dragged me straight home. All the way back, he chided me for my careless words, and then there it was—a slap on my left cheek for causing trouble. Back then, it was a normal practice to reprimand one's child physically, hoping a fearful memory would deter the same error forever. I cried for hours, more for losing my lovely silver sandals. I did not understand how any of it was my fault. The entire episode left me confused.

Gurmeet was untraceable for the next fifteen days, and I refused to say a word about it. I constantly spoke to my dear Ganesh, like I always did, seeking his help this one last time.

'Please Ganeshji, please do not be so angry with me. I know I've not kept my promise. The echoes of all these whispers and thoughts surround me like a whirlwind I cannot escape. They force me to speak. I may not know what I'm doing but you know me better than myself. Please do something.' The girl returned in a fortnight, bringing a sigh of relief for the parents and my dad's guilt but this event left me adrift for a while, windswept in a sea of emotions yet isolated all the same.

By then, along with the many names—Maa, Devi Maa, Kali Maa, and all other forms of the primordial mother—people touched my feet for the divine intervention they perceived in me. They added a new suffix to my name at thirteen—ji, separating me from the normal, even though no one at home adulated me.

A strong wind blew me into a zone I could not fathom or assimilate. I felt the need to ground myself. I had much to learn. For hours on end, I sat in silence. I needed direction and answers. I did not wish for any separation and was open to ideas, stimulating exchanges, and conversations with friends and peers. Yet, in this division, I also found a new opportunity to listen, to ask questions, and to argue with my father's literati friends. One of them spoke of a well-known eye surgeon who gave it all up to pursue a common interest we shared—palmistry and astrology. For a week, his name flashed up in different contexts: Dr Yogesh Mishra.

It was time I addressed all the ambiguous questions piling up in my little head.

Listen . . .
when you have a spare moment,
do me a favour.
Take a handful of clay
knead it
mould it
make a two-sided marionette.
One is you
the other is me.
In time, break them both
add some more clay
knead it

mould it
make a two-sided marionette,
one just like me
the other just like you.
In the making,
fragments of me will melt into you,
and
tiny morsels of you will carve into me.
When you have a spare moment,
do me a favour.

4
Engraved in Gold

I yearned for something more—a better education on how thoughts manifested, how an intangible force influenced my words, and how I may hold a simple prayer without the anxiety of losing myself in it. I feared for my sanity every time someone positioned me differently or glorified my name. I, the one who acquainted the young and old with their futures, needed guidance to navigate her present.

Gaur Saheb, a close friend of my father, understood my need for support. He offered to introduce me to Dr Yogesh Mishra, an eminent eye surgeon who retired in his mid-fifties to pursue the study of astrology and the human mind. The two men shared a warm friendship and often discussed literature, science, and the intricacies of analytical and predictive astrology.

So, one lively spring morning in 1978, when red and orange bougainvillaea vines stretched across the sandy dunes, we drove to the surgeon's house in Gaur Saheb's car. On the way, we spoke about Dr Mishra's keen knowledge of Indian astrology and his shift of profession from an eye surgeon to phenomenology and metaphysics. At the entrance to the house, I pressed my palm onto the tall wooden door of a two-storeyed building, eyeing an engraved name sign in antique gold that read: Dr Yogesh Mishra. A kind-looking middle-aged lady ushered us in. We walked into a room lit with three fluorescent tubes, one in the middle and two on either side of the ceiling. To my left were two old wooden armchairs with a small desk lamp by the corner. The other two walls were clustered with scores of hard-cover books on wooden bookcases.

A cherub-faced, ageing gentleman, with a visceral feel about him, sat at an old teak desk. He greeted Gaur Saheb, and then pointed to the green, large, cushioned seats opposite him, gesturing for us to sit.

I folded my hands in namaskar and bowed in respect before I sat on the low chair. Dr Mishra stood up at leisure and looked at me through his glasses for what seemed like a lifetime. His large round eyes shone like two small golden eggs through his rimmed glasses. I shrank further into my seat with his tall frame over me but didn't miss his shifting expressions. I wanted to giggle at his odd appearance; a forehead wider than most I had seen, a silvery moustache, and a small rosy face.

Gaur Sahib did most of the talking, telling him how I picked up vibrations in a thought to assess a person's past and future and that most of my predictions came true. He also spoke of my intuitive abilities and interest in palmistry.

I said little during that first meeting. 'I am currently studying the *Laghu Parashari* among other texts for a better understanding of astrology and Indian astronomy,' I said. Dr Mishra then noted my date of birth and we decided to come back another day.

Two weeks later, Gaur Sahib and I sat in his study once again. It was mid-afternoon, the sun shone brightly through the sash-bar window behind Dr Mishra's desk, and we had tea and snacks. After a general conversation, the eye surgeon began pacing around the room. Every ten seconds, he glanced in my direction, perhaps for evidence of the thoughts entering his mind. After all the scrutiny, he blurted, 'You are *swayam siddha*—the one who has an inner knowing. You know all the answers to your questions.'

'Huh?' I said, while staring at him wide-eyed. As he walked back to his side of the desk, I felt a tingle through my pores. It felt like I was absorbing something through my skin, from the air, the room's brilliance and the stillness around this man.

Dr Mishra spoke, 'You are the quintessence of the universal mother. If you wish, Nirmala, you will be proficient in the occult sciences and the metaphysical aspects of this universe. I see your destiny in serving humanity.'

I stood up, eyes darting straight at him. Leisurely folding both hands together, while straightening my back, I said, 'I am a simple girl. I have no fears. Each time someone seeks information, I ask Ganesh for help, while also promising him I will not ask again. The truth is I have broken this trust several times. I detest lies and do not wish to mislead people. I am so sure Ganesh does not like telling lies either. This is my problem. I am looking for a solution.'

The professor's expression softened as he looked at me and Gaur Saheb with a gentle smile. He nodded and pointed to the same plump embroidered cushion on the chair, asking me to sit back and relax. I opened my mouth to speak again but I caught the kindness and patience in his eyes and fumbled for more words.

He spoke again, quiet yet firm, 'You, Nirmala, a young girl now but a woman soon. You are a form of the universal mother. Like the rest of us, you too are here with a purpose. A purpose I see in the lines of your palms where the boundaries of the heart and mind melt into each other. A rare phenomenon.'

'But I want to be an actor, join the theatre, and be a pretty bride one day,' I interrupted.

'A thousand brides will come for guidance to you, my dear. It is time to recognise your own uniqueness. To know yourself so you may know and assist others. You will master the hidden if you wish.'

'I love wearing pretty dresses. I just love colours.' I protested.

'Most girls your age wish the same. Drop it. It is not for you, Devi. What makes you so involved in a play, an enticing illusion, when there is so much reality waiting to unfold within you?'

'I love playing the sitar and laughing with my friends.'

'You can still do that Nirmala, but you must choose your purpose before it all.'

'But . . . why me?'

'Why not? You have an opportunity to acknowledge yourself, accept your destiny, and walk ahead with courage.'

'But . . .?' I said and then stopped. A roaring silence followed.

'Why not Nirmala . . . why not?' Dr Mishra's words sliced through my rumbling stomach, and I shuffled uncomfortably. I sat stunned, my whole being vibrating, unfolding, whispering and trying to tear through the many folds, to reveal something. His question echoed through my bones. I closed my eyes in search of the answers, perhaps written under some hidden stone in indelible ink.

A narrow path revealed itself, and I realised what I already knew. I knew Ganesh was never angry with me. Every time I spoke to my best friend, I felt nurtured, safe, and fearless but never tormented. I sat there, exposed, vulnerable, and uncertain with what I did not comprehend as a teenager. Yet, I also knew I could believe this man, trust him and learn from him.

I could not shy away anymore. I had met my guru.

That night, I dreamt of walking through a dense tropical forest, using my arms and legs to hack through an overlaid rich vegetation. Disorderly branches, intimidating stalks, gigantic rubber leaves, and mesmeric buttress roots cleverly closed in to trip the wayward traveller. I knew I had to keep walking. I had to find my map.

On waking up, I stayed a while thinking of the rendezvous between the night and my wayward thoughts. Many questions flooded back, and contradictions surfaced too. If constant change is inevitable, what are the possibilities of standing steady in this colossal movement of stars, planets, a million suns and moons?

Gradually, I learned to hold steady, to fall back on my own convictions when I walked into tunnels, trusting none other than myself. My father always reminded me that the quality of our daily interactions with one another determines the depth of a human being. Every conversation, each collective discussion, and each moment is special. It builds character, creating generosity and open-mindedness to walk better in an ever-evolving diverse world.

It also took time for me to understand the word—guru. I believe our eyes are the foremost teacher—the guru. Have you ever observed a baby watching this world with absolute intent? It does not blink quickly, and in that process, thousands of pictures are compiled in the brain, mind, and body. These images carve our thinking, likes and dislikes for a whole lifetime. And then nature's efforts at every step, symbolise a guru (a teacher). Our parents and peers are teachers too who influence us deeply yet there comes a time when we meet the one who shows us the mirror, lights the path and enables our efforts like no other.

Since the day I met my guru, I walk each day, aware of an intent, an effort and a determination towards the next step. Personally, a guru is an *ahsaas*—a vibrant feeling, a constant reflection, never fading, always present, pushing me forward on a journey within.

The guru gives,
I shine
like a star in the sky.
The guru teaches
reverence and effort.
I find divinity.
In the magnificent whole
The guru is whole
in knowing, knowledge, and intent.
Your light
nourishes my existence.
Guru, you are whole.
Oh my guru,
I mirror you
in this world.
I spread the radiance
I absorb
from you, my guru.
I am your light, O guru
and you
are my identity.

5

The Axis of Effort

Whenever I travel to Ajmer, my birthplace, I enjoy taking a detour ten kilometres north to sit by the banks of a mystical lake in Pushkar and watch the sun disappearing into the twilight. Pushkar Lake harbours a few smouldering myths of India and on a full moon night, these ancient flames rise, spreading their arms as they come alive to protect guarded traditions. A million bodies take a dip in its waters with faith in those who have lived before us. With their beliefs spanning a thousand centuries, the hopes and wishes of this indigenous race remain as conditioned as history can remember. Yet, I feel a sense of relief sitting by the lake and amuse myself with the sights that shock, mesmerise, and lure the unassuming traveller to these lands in the hope of some divine revelation.

And then I wonder if one should follow the historical myth or question its validity in the current context. And how do I find some common ground? A new world where both may exist in the present, walking ahead in a redesigned, reinvented, more sustainable co-existence into the future.

In this ancestral lake, teeming with folklore, parables, and wisdom, I have also pondered on what it means to have the privilege of friendly guides, efficient maps, and effective teachers. Where does one find them? I believe they come unspoken and leave unheard. These gentle prompts are not self-proclaimed knowers of it all. No. They lie hidden in the intimacy of a seed, veiled from the glare of the outward eye.

A guru is the axis of effort. The cause or the beginning of effort, a gentle force nudging one towards an efficient performance. The mother is the first guru to every newborn in all of creation, whether a calf, fawn, duckling, or a human. An infant absorbs from the mother. It imbibes the quality instilled by her. And then there are other teachers, fundamental in the brick-laying process of a child who learns to walk, run, wish, pray and think.

Dr Yogesh Mishra unearthed a dormant seed in me when I was barely fourteen. He started a process, an effort to direct my thought process from being scattered to relative clarity and recognition. I visited Dr Mishra once a week in Jawahar Nagar on the outskirts of Jaipur. When I did not get a scooter or car ride from someone in the family, it took me forty-five minutes to walk to his place which doubled as his home and ashram. Here he taught astrology, logic, and discipline in spirituality to a group of young boys.

I remember spending the first two hours learning the theory in astrology and then debating on metaphysics with a man well into his sixties who abandoned a scientific career to understand the mysteries of precision and unity within the cosmic world. He taught all of us the finer details of theoretical astrology but maintained that I learn the science behind sound. He encouraged me to study the Yajur Ved, an ancient treatise of mantras. So, I taught myself Sanskrit to understand and then recite hundreds of coded Sanskrit phrases. I began chanting mantras with no prior understanding of pitch, sound, or frequency.

I sometimes wondered why Dr Yogesh Mishra insisted on me learning mantras when he hardly chanted any himself. It did not interest him, he had said, yet he asserted his opinion like he knew it all. I thought that was so illogical. I resisted every time he prompted me, and defiantly raised these doubts with him. I was a teenager with a loud voice and cared little for what others thought of me. Dr Mishra's pestering annoyed me. But all my resistance failed as my heart felt a magnetic pull like none other. The attraction was so strong that it left me with little choice. It was as if I had known Dr Mishra since the beginning of time and now, he had returned. I simply loved listening to his soft voice, and the common sense behind his words. We discussed for hours, and it built my confidence because healthy debate challenges the mind. It makes one think, reflect and question without reservations.

Yogesh Mishra shared parables to get the point across, repeating the same story several times so that it impressed deeper and deeper upon my being. These stories often help now when I need them to counsel others. One such story that influenced me deeply was about an ascetic who lived up the mountains in a cave, seated in samadhi, oblivious to the outer world. One day, his student, sitting close by on a hill, contemplated on a cloudless sky and had a vision. Circles of different colours flashed in and out of his sight. He rubbed his eyes to make sure he was not daydreaming. The flashing colours started as a dot and grew as he watched. The brightness of every colour captivated him. He realised these were hundreds of rainbows emerging in the sky. One rainbow circle grew larger and larger till it gave way to the smaller ones appearing within it. He ran to the meditating sage and tried everything to arouse him out of his deep state. As soon as his teacher opened his eyes, the student excitedly described the scene in the sky. He said, 'You must experience it before you miss this rare phenomenon.'

The sage listened. When the student calmed down, he smiled, speaking softly, 'What you are watching on the outside and getting so excited about has been happening inside of me, all along. I have witnessed within me the profundity of a thousand rainbows much brighter than all you say.'

This story served a purpose. Initially, it worked like magic, turning my perspective upside down and leaving me with no choice but to gradually discover my truth in it. I began the long journey of living this story. I sat for hours chanting mantras, or staying quiet, occasionally feeling more aligned, aware and conscious. As months passed, I often wondered if I would follow these impulses to discover more of myself. It took years to become steady in the exploration, and now I wish for young ones to find the courage and enough rebellion in their bones to dive deeper into their own selves.

In the winter of 1979, I looked forward to meeting my mentor, sometimes twice a week. Every time I walked into the courtyard, young Brahmin boys, students of the ashram deliberately stood up, bowed in mock respect, and sang in chorus.

'Here enters the all-knowing Devi Maa—divine mother!' they shouted, clapping all the way till I entered the professor's room. They laughed at my accent, emulating the way I pronounced Sanskrit phonetics. In the beginning, I shouted back at them or laughed with them, but the teasing made me sad some days and I complained.

When I reflect on those days, I am reminded of my naivety and a deceptive separation in the social order. These boys strongly believed in their birthright and privilege whereas I had to fight for my place. Yet, Dr Mishra paid no attention to the name-calling. He never once reprimanded them or fed into their ignorance. Holding me steady, he dismissed my complaints, constantly reminding me to believe in nothing but myself. As my guru, he touched upon an unspoken understanding, patience, and the strength of an old banyan tree. I was his student in equal measure with the young men, yet our interaction needed a few words. He could access my thoughts, and I absorbed immensely from the wisdom in his eyes.

I went on to study the intricacies of theoretical Indian astrology which included astronomy and astral combinations, and the stars that influence birth, life, and synchronicity. For nearly two years, I observed the phases of the moon and their effect on the personalities of all creatures. I was naturally intuitive, but now I learnt to combine a birth chart with my insights. I also studied the influences of diverse geographical environments and social demographics on the human mind.

Dr Mishra often commented, 'The world of astronomy is grandeur in all its colours. Each time I dive into it, it invites me deeper in, much like the intricate perfection of a naked eye when put under a microscope.'

I did not doubt him there and learned that any unknown aspect remains magical and elusive only till one discovers its workings. With my guru's encouragement, I studied Sanskrit texts, like the *Mansagari* and *Taajik Neelkanthi*. I matured at reading charts, increasingly relying on mathematical calculations. I wrote nothing down but experimented at every step and when I found evidence, I knew it deep in my bones. It was a crucial step at the time although I do not use charts anymore because I have absorbed most of it.

Dr Mishra explained how the farmers of yesteryears were intelligent enough to study the position of the planets, allowing them to sow seeds at an opportune moment. Similarly, sailors studied the direction of the stars to correctly navigate and arrive at their destination. However, in recent generations, there has been hardly any preference or research into Indian astrology, despite evidence indicating that modern astronomy stems from traditional branches of metaphysical study. There is a clear connection between astral combinations, the phases of the moon, and the interdependence of all life on planet earth. This knowledge has enriched the lives of those few who studied it.

My teacher taught me to look at 'knowledge' as it is, bound in its extensive contexts of geography, culture, social status, history, religion, politics, and most of all, the passing of time. Information and its comprehension develop and evolve to the changing needs of its environment. As and when major shifts occur in the relative state, a dire need for substantial research arises every now and then or it stagnates. Thus, adapting to the current environment is the key to innovation.

When the boys teased more, Dr Mishra often walked out of his room quietly to announce, 'You, Devi Kalyani are more than you think. A reservoir of knowledge lies folded within your little mind, waiting to unfold as you dig deeper.'

I mostly shook my head, brushing him off. But he spoke adamantly, 'We all hold neatly folded treasures from past impressions, waiting to unfold in this or subsequent lifetimes. It is your choice to look at a map and follow its directions or turn away into the wilderness. And Nirmala, you are swayam siddha. You just do not know it yet.

These were complex words I did not comprehend but knew how much Dr Mishra supported me. When the constant taunting from the boys upset me, I lay my anxious head on a pillow wondering about the words my guru spoke. Often, I woke to a dream and saw him smiling in the blushing pink light of another dawn, whispering, 'Nirmala, you naturally know of your own intimate being. We all do. My job is to remind you of that till you experience and realise this phenomenon yourself. This is the knowing in knowledge.'

Dr Mishra pushed me to think beyond the perceived vision. He questioned anything I said, teaching me to hunt beyond the limited ideas of a conditioned brain and the external eye. This strengthened my principle to lead and not follow, to innovate not imitate and to constantly understand the shift in time and space. I have voiced my opinion for years now. The religiously literate Brahmins quote from ancient texts, expecting masses to follow concepts that are approximately five thousand years old. They imitate the ways of the ancient sages with complete ignorance of the evolved, globalised environments of today.

Yogesh Mishra also taught me the complexities of astrology and how one could study the art to understand the self. I scanned my birth chart, discovering more about my purpose in this lifetime. For example, Saturn in its own third house and Jupiter in the fifth house influenced me since birth, pushing me to think more along abstract concepts of being, identity, space and knowing.

In time, the mystery of a guru comes to an end. I broke through the cement to undo my habits and soon a new rebellion surfaced. I discovered the dilemmas of an independent thought. At this stage, a strange brevity entered, and I saw my guru's limitations too. He was a genius at astrology but had no understanding of the depth and power of a mantra.

It was time to take responsibility for my own growth and I did.

Listen . . .
you are a piece of the midday sun,
at times here,
often there,
and sometimes you disappear.

I constantly run after you,
hoping to catch you someday.
Yet, when I am in the
twilight of life
you will have to face me whole.
Then,
You will embrace me,
because,
I am the horizon . . . isn't it?

6

Nine Nights

It took four nine-day phases for me to anchor myself firmly in silence. A defiant mind, previous success and a longing for the unknown, pushed me forward. I felt a tiny green shoot spread its roots within me ever so softly. My words became more measured, predictions more precise, and diction of the Sanskrit language more refined. The mind moved at a much faster pace, filtering every thought travelling through the air. During this time, I read classic literature, Sanskrit theology texts on the feminine such as *Devimahatmaya*, and postmodern philosophers like Acharya Rajneesh, gathering much information and knowledge.

It took another three years of silence, till I felt a renewed awareness. Noise played on my nerves and the slightest disturbance in our quiet home put me on edge. Nothing went amiss; I could hear sounds a mile away. My senses became stronger, colours more vivid, and taste much more distilled. I filtered smells to the point of irritation or to the zenith of a fragrant delicacy. I did not doubt my feelings. I never do. Every bit of scattered energy accumulated like golden lava within me, becoming a mass of solid gold, molten and smooth. With this profound strength, I discovered the nuances of invoking fire and performed ceremonies while chanting mantras with a depth that was new to me.

By the age of twenty-one, I adapted to a world that was different to mine. In a sea of people, I stood alone at a level I cannot explain. I developed patience and tolerance for the diversity in my environment and learnt more restraint as compared to the habitual mind. This brought in a significant shift, anchoring me steadily within my body. A fleeting thought was now more essential, the intellect far more alert, which allowed for accurate calculations and flash decisions. A strange endurance kicked in just as it does for any sportsperson who becomes consistent in one's dedicated sport and nothing, well, almost nothing can touch it. No one at home or otherwise questioned me as I led the brigade. It was a high with a choice—a free will to ride that wave or to crash under its weight.

Once during the nine-day silent phase, my youngest sister, Seetu, was jumping up and down on the bed. I entered the room, looked at her, shook my head, and shouted out aloud, 'Seetu, you are so skinny and if you keep jumping like that, you will disappear one day.'

Seetu came to a sudden halt. With both hands over her mouth and wide-eyed, she muttered, 'Baby, you have just broken your silence!' I squirmed and then went back into being quiet. I worked on the word 'guilt' for the remaining five days and wrote about it in my journal. With this incident, I learnt to let go of the last moment. It is gone, you cannot rewind it. It is the mind that finds comfort in the organised moment and the memory of the past. It does not like surprises. I got over it soon and instead discovered beauty in the spontaneity of expression. I made a conscious decision to function through instinct and flexibility rather than the rigidity of a habituated mind.

In the next four years of my practice, I also learnt the difference between reaction and response. One autumn morning, in the middle of the nine-day fasting event, I sat by the large open window in my room, engrossed in the book, *Autobiography of a Yogi*, when all of a sudden, something hit my forearm. The force had the same intensity as a hammer hitting a panel of iron. My head reeled, and I sat up straight as the intensity of the knock numbed me. The pain shot through my shoulder, and I cringed. Yet, a force within me watched it all happen and I did not cry aloud. Not one gasp, not one shriek of pain and no whining either.

My brother Shankar and his friends were playing cricket, when the solid leather-covered ball flew straight through the open window and smashed into the side of my left arm. Soon enough, all the boys rushed into my room while Maa shouted, sending them back out. She assumed I was lying unconscious. In response, I sat upright within a minute, waving my other hand to gesture that I wasn't hurt.

As I lay back, I felt a numbing pain and cried myself to sleep. After a few hours, I woke, feeling sore in the body, yet strangely triumphant. I did not react in the situation. I had discovered a tensile strength I never felt before. It permeated my mind and my being.

That night I wrote in my diary, 'Silence infiltrates the skin through a million pores, and travels to the bloodstream. It then envelopes me like a shawl on a winter morning. It imprints an understated permanence whereas a word once spoken expands into oblivion, becoming redundant in the creation of a new word. It is temporary.'

By the summer of 1985, after another eight such self-disciplining periods, I began experimenting with mantras and their use in the occult. This practice of chanting also helped immensely during the long stretches of silence. '*Mantro mananat trayate iti mantraha*' is a common Sanskrit phrase which serves as a basic explanation of mantras to any seeker. It means that a formula of high-frequency sounds when repeatedly chanted also induces a proportional impact on its environment. People often conceptualise mantras as parts of speech or grammar and try desperately to dissect a cluster of sounds through vocabulary. However, the magic of any mantra lies in the subtle knowledge of sound. Just as prescribed medicine impacts the body, the frequency of a specific sound influences the mind, different layers of the body, and the immediate environment.

Mantras broadly classify as symbols and clusters of resonating vibrations that turn effective when repeatedly uttered within a specific tempo. The phonemes create a higher, volatile frequency like waves expanding in concentric circles covering more space as they rotate. This expansion of frequency protects the utterer, his or her space, and the environment, to then spread further out to the seas, the skies, the planet, the universe, and the cosmos. A static pattern turns dynamic. This also explains the fire ceremonies I perform which involve invocations of specific mantras to aid a purposeful resolution.

I first dived into the esoteric world at thirteen, when I began reading periodic journals on the subject, Sanskrit texts, and interpretations of *Vedic Sahitya*. The *Yajur Ved Sahitya* states that a mantra chanted in repetition with the right intent and intonation creates currents of vibrations in the environment. When repeated one hundred thousand times, a sound wave strengthens in proportion to the number of relative utterances. This generates a high-frequency field and a sound barrier that protects the utterer. So, after chanting a mantra repeatedly for one hundred and twenty-five thousand times, I started performing a fire ceremony to mark the end of a cycle of chants.

I believe listening and reading are prerequisites for experiencing something significant. So, I started experimenting with what I was reading. Chanting for long hours, I frequently watched myself travelling and swaying in different realms even though I sat upright in the lotus position. This is *anubhav*, the individual subtle feeling unique to each one of us. It is important to discern between feeling and thought, wherein feeling is much finer of the two. A lingering feeling creates a thought—a sad, ugly, prejudiced, clear, and bold thought. But feelings are also tricky, elusive creatures; their origins mostly lie in deep-seated desires, influences, desperations, and impressions. So, my silences enabled a clarity where I could dive deeper and deeper to excavate the spontaneity of a feeling and then believe in it with conviction.

This is where observing and then re-educating the mind becomes so crucial. The discipline in silence allows space and time for introspection. It questions, criticises, discerns, understands, and then expands a position to the extreme, ultimately rendering it redundant. Silence has its own aim, its own mission, and its own purpose. It unravels knowing and deconstructs inherited patterns and habits of the mind. Because silence shuts away the humdrum of the surface, it opens access to hidden passages. It constantly sifts feelings and thoughts, hoovering away the dust, thus leaving all the stored pictures and impressions bare and exposed. It leaves the seeker alone in it all with an urgent choice—to own responsibility or to look away.

I did follow my sister into the nine days of fasting, but not without questioning its relevance. We may not recognise this on starting a new project, but nothing begins without reason and the information we initially have, also dilutes and expands with environments. So, could I trust anything at all? I needed evidence and the only way to get that was to experiment with it. The more I went back to silence, the more I trusted it, and with time, a steady shift occurred, and my knowing became stronger. I carried the discipline of maun for the next thirty-five years, marking it as 'a preferred silence amidst sounds' for thirty-six days on my calendar. No retreats, no caves, and no isolation. I entered the arena of silence in my noisy, busy, immediate environment.

Each nine-day period of silence filled a gap somewhere in the mind. Because I was not talking; I was listening better. Because I was not eating, I understood my anatomy better. I got a handle on greed and how it manifests from scattered thoughts, indulgence, and influences. Because I was not involved in communication, I observed situations way better from a distance, discovering a much wider lens into perspective. And because I continued chanting within, I understood my mind better. This was a gift . . . a knowing. I observed the preciousness of words and the frivolity in them. I learnt to deal 'with' and not 'with-out'. Silence amongst others demands adaptability and flexibility with little expectations and therefore differs from the silence of an isolated cave.

The quarterly nine-day fasting periods carry a universal appeal even though the concept lies buried in tradition and myth. These days occur at significant lunisolar phases in the Vedic almanac with the first period in February; a time of conception which happens when form and energy collide, an intense force becomes available to all forms of life on earth and thus creativity manifests. At this time of the year, a concentrated dynamism creates a new abundance. This shy, vulnerable, delicate stage is a time for introspection mostly pursued by a serious seeker.

Next is spring, when Hindu communities all over the world commonly celebrate *Vaasantik Navratri* where feminine energy or life force gives birth to a bud. She creates and all of nature bears evidence to this phenomenon in the tiny buds that emerge out of the womb, bearing life and a promise for growth and progress.

The third set of nine-day fasts begins at the peak of the monsoon when the preciousness of water nourishes the earth. It sustains all of life. In folklore, seers regard water as the foremost teacher. This is because a real teacher is one who earns respect through effort and never proclaims it; just like water. It just flows. It is another period of introspection veiled from common society. A time for observing the privilege of teachers in nature—the sun, moon, ants, fish, and fellow humans. This is an ideal time to access the intelligence and wisdom of mentors or a guru; to imbibe their discipline and will in order to find the courage to walk more independently.

The last nine-day period of the year occurs in autumn, concluding a cycle and preparing the soil for renewed creativity. The decaying and falling of leaves. A reshuffle of the three previous stages takes place. This is a time for reflections on the past and preparations for the new while also accepting limitations. Humans are one aspect of nature. Nature persists, not humans. Thus, each year these nine days offer one more opportunity to shift back into sync with nature. A time to celebrate change, to witness it, and to flow with it.

Like most people who observe these fasts, I too read a mythological narrative, a *katha*, throughout the nine days of fasting. This particular story is centred around a conflict between deities and demons. Over the last forty-odd years of repeatedly reading it, I have envisioned, lived, and understood it differently. This katha grows a little more in me, each time I read it and I find much evidence of the human predicament in it. Broadly, it speaks of a vicious battle between the two faces of a human—a demonic being *(asura)* versus a divine being *(devas)*. It depicts how the demonic forces of greed, control, lust, and envy heavily dominate the lighter traits of integrity, courage, honesty, empathy, and compassion. All these forces may seem elusive or unreal, but in reality, they are more real and enduring than the human who comes under their influence. Millions of humans come and go but these powers thrive. History shows us the stubborn persistence of these forces.

In this story, powerful demons dictate and control the universe, forcing the devas to unite because they fear extinction. The devas meditate as a collective force, emitting streams of flames to create a formidable energy—the primordial feminine, a *devi*, who independently contains within herself their combined forces. They entrust a divine woman with the impossible task of destroying the demons one by one. She assumes an autonomous position.

The first demon, Madhukaitambh, represents honey that enters the conscious human through the ear, flattering the mind into sleep, laziness, and complacency. The next, Dhoomralochan, embodies external influences and smoke screens that cast ugly shadows on clarity and discrimination. This powerful feminine kills them both and there is temporary relief when gratitude amplifies and greed subsides. A moment filled with content. However, the cyclical nature of nature prevails, with attraction intensifying. Raging in lust and wanting to consume a divine beauty, another demon emerges. Chand-Mund represents beauty that is skin deep or on the surface. It masks an illusion and hides reality, thus crushing conscious thought. The feminine energy kills this demon, but the next force is not far behind. The demons are emphatic. They resurface, returning more powerful and invincible as a demon named Asakt after which pride and arrogance follow with Shumb Nishumb. Trampling these three tendencies, the feminine force then encounters the worst kind of demon in Raktbeej which literally means 'one drop of blood in the form of a seed.' The story goes that while fighting with the primordial feminine, each time a drop of this demon's blood touched the earth, it created a new warrior. So, to counter the attack, the devi transforms herself into another powerful feminine force, Kali, who swallows every drop of the demon's blood before it touches the ground. This is deeply symbolic because in doing so she breaks the obvious cycles of violence much before these seeds (of blood) take root. Finally, this feminine force faces the most powerful monster, Mahishasur, who represents egotism and self-delusion. Each time she kills them, they re-emerge taking a new form. This part of the story serves as a reminder for all to check their resurfacing egos. The devi also projects endless divine forms, like knowledge, compassion, and wisdom, ultimately defeating the half-human, half-bull demon and restoring peace to the devas or the calmer mind. Mythically, the male devas confer this feminine force with the highest principle comprising the three aspects: creation, preservation, and destruction. She intervenes to restore balance in the cosmos.

Each time I read this story, one more layer unfolds. I treat it as a useful map that I can use in times of confusion. The analogy of Raktbeej resonates in me deeply as it symbolises the struggle we all face—the seeds of thoughts and desires that manifest and develop roots day after day, year after year and lifetime after lifetime. Humans confront this demon in most interactions. It is akin to the spider's web; a web of fears, phobias, control, greed, and lust. A hapless, confused mind gets caught in this intricate maze unexpectedly.

It is important to constantly remind oneself of the power of weight, and what it does. Weight pulls us down. Have you noticed when a child makes a wish, she looks at the sky? When the same child is in doubt or ashamed, she looks down. And because the earth is in the middle, with our feet constantly on it, we absorb the heavy attributes and aspects more easily.

So, what are my chances here and what is the saving grace? I believe awareness is the key. When we become aware of our fears, we understand them better. In time, with much effort, the mind gradually adapts, shifts, and starts thinking independently of habit. We understand where weaker ideas originate from. Silence facilitates this shift in the subconscious because it persists and expands. Devoid of an inexhaustible array of words, silence enables a steady awareness.

Shilpi, a young radio journalist, once asked me if the chatter of the mind when one is quiet was the same as talking aloud. It is an interesting question. Speaking aloud requires immense energy and creates a peripheral vibration within and in the surrounding boundary, whereas the internal use of the same words involves none of those aspects. When we are quiet, the tongue and lips remain still. The mind is not reacting to another person's thoughts. There is no interference with externals—with the conditioned answer, with what another expects, or with the desire to outperform. In that process of a quiet chatter, you conserve the energy used for speaking, discussing, or arguing. In time, the habit changes, and the frequency alters. Because of this non-performance and a rush of energy, the speed of one's thoughts becomes a thousand times faster.

This is a frustrating stage though, as it contradicts the word 'silence'. The mind falters in confusion and goes into denial. Most people give up here and distance themselves further and further away from the ones who are dedicated. In addition, human memory is so short-lived it forgets that earth time does not constrain the journey of the self. Time becomes their biggest hurdle. We want it now. Therefore, I insist that patience is the key. Acceptance of one's wayward thoughts eventually allows a transition into areas of filtered thought.

Discipline endures far more consistently from a longing for creative freedom rather than the rigidity of strict training.

Creativity does not command discipline, rather, it forces an attraction impossible to resist. It invites, offering a different flavour. It flows in reverse, from the inside to the outside . . . from a creative core to the external world. It creates a fresh lease of life turning a seeker into the 'disciple' of a discipline, study, or sport. You become your own best friend.

When I contemplate quietly, my mind processes faster and the recurrent thought vibrates at a higher frequency. It unfolds a layer, making space for something new; something not taught before. It is in reversal to all the ideologies that discipline us into following. This fresh space creates havoc with the complexities of the habituated mind. And if I persist, the process of 'unlearning' begins. The punched-in, fixed patterns give way to an individual idea, an innovative thought, and an independent, often rebellious decision.

Eventually, each one finds their own logic, evidence and madness in silence. Practised for years, it gave me the required tools, one by one, to disconnect with the spoken word so I could re-phrase my words to speak and discuss again with a renewed consideration for what I know or do not know. It paves the way for a constructive argument where either you make me understand something I do not know or recognise what I know. In both ways, an expansion takes place and knowledge evolves.

My guru often reminded me of an age-old precept. He said, 'If a person sitting in a cave dies in deep introspection, her/his body made up of the five elements, returns to the earth . . . but the contemplative thought manifests, it carries forward, finding its destiny through another being in a body.'

How does that happen? Through the practice of silence, I access vibrations in a thought much before they turn vocal. Before one asks a question, I answer. Journalists interviewing me have observed this and often commented on it. This is not magic or any special ability. Each one of us can access these frequencies. Thoughts are almost like things, just as one hands an orange to a friend and takes it back, so does one pass a useful or useless thought to the next person and takes it back. Thoughts move with a dominant force, creating and destroying as they travel. A thought travels faster than the speed of light. But then how many of us step out of the set algorithm to enter the threshold of an expanded ability? Yet when we do, and a person calls you just as you thought of her/him, we call it telepathy. We have labelled it; we choose to accept it and not explore further.

In February 2015, my mother passed away, and I gave up the periods of maun. No one understood my silent gestures the way she did. Communication with the external world became a tedious task after her. My mother was the most crucial anchor on this ride into the esoteric.

   I think of her often after a long day. Lying in bed, tears slide down my cheek, streaking the white pillowcase with greyish dots. The silence of a night becomes relevant in that moment. I pen another poem honouring the divine feminine—motherhood. I read it repeatedly. The beauty of a mother astounds me.

Maa, you show me
how to embrace all
with a healing touch.
Maa, in your creation,
divinity is whole.
Divinity, you are whole.

Maa, I gather your radiance.
It illuminates
my path.
Maa, you are beautiful
in a formless creation.
I am your form.
Maa, simple as you are,
with deep reverence
I kiss your feet.

7
Echoes without a Whisper

I listen to my footsteps while walking in the woods, especially on an auburn autumn afternoon. Crisp, brittle, fallen leaves play havoc on the path. The obvious crunch, crunch and crackle and then another crunch unsettles the quietness. I tiptoe. I am infringing on the stillness, leaving behind a loud impression. I wait. I strain my ears to hear the faintest sound, and my breath suspends for a moment or two.

Intimidating tall trees and menacing weeds intrude my path. Persisting roots snake their way under my feet, a winding river follows me faithfully, and irreverent clouds shadow the changing blues. Collectively, they merge thoughts of the past into the present to create projections of the future. I drop a smooth grey stone into the river and watch. A small homocentric ripple begins to travel outwards, continuously expanding into the periphery. It reminds me of the same force and frequency that carries a mind-thought forward into an unknown atmosphere. So, I wonder . . . if a thought carries forward, what is its compass and where does it go?

I imagine a thought entering my mind just like a sudden ripple emerges in quiet waters. I watch a singular thought grow and expand into a circular wave. Thoughts exist in the atmosphere, and because I am an intrinsic part of nature, whatever exists on the earth reveals itself in my thoughts too. When a thought crosses my mind, concentric vibrations arise in the *manas* (the processing mind). This one thought travels to create a string of consequent thoughts. Just as air is the medium for sound and breath is the vehicle for feeling, similarly, an active or passive mind is the vehicle for a variety of thoughts; positive or negative thoughts, happy or sad thoughts, and idle or productive thoughts. Often a wandering thought surprises the mind, leading to a eureka moment or a brilliant idea. If one focuses on that thought, it expands, and the vibration settles into the mind. It manifests.

Imagine a large piece of fabric with its warp and weft woven with thoughts that intermingle, connect, play, fight, heal, indulge, empathise, and damage without one spoken word. It is a complex world, yet an invisible force. An understated intelligence, alive and living. A thought is as solid as stone. It has form, colour, weight, size, shape, and quality. It is a dynamic force generated through vibrations in the subtle consciousness.

Just as heat, light, and electric waves affect the outer environment, thought waves affect the conscious mind. In varying degrees, each one experiences the vibrations in a thought subconsciously or unconsciously. Every thought sent out to another travels in a vibration that never perishes rather it continues to vibrate every particle in the universe. Similarly, every impulse of the mind and each rising thought passes on to the cells in the human body. Cells are in a direct relationship with the mind. The condition of the mind affects each body cell. Confused, negative, depressed, and anxious thoughts are all transmitted through the nerves into every cell of the body. Panic-stricken cells vibrate at a lower frequency, affecting the nervous system. Thoughts thus can cause imbalances in the body.

In contrast, constructive thoughts have the power to renew, transform, and build. A thought moves like a wireless message, manifesting with tremendous speed. Exploring the higher regions of the mind allows the realisation of this immense power in a thought. It enables an occultist to hear distant voices, see remote objects, send messages, and heal a person from long distances. The following case study explains the rippling effect of a thought and the collective thought vibrations that drift in the environment.

In September 2012, Sarika, a friend in Australia, telephoned, informing me of her sister Ruchi's deteriorating condition after liver failure. Doctors at King's College Hospital, London, had given up on the case and the news devastated Sarika. She called me for some alternative intervention. I tuned into the intense emotions Sarika felt for her sister. Soon, I felt this strong connection as my own. At the peak of this feeling, I empathised with the pain and the helpless state Ruchi was in. Picking up the information, I tapped into Ruchi's thoughts, who was lying on a hospital bed in a coma. I sent out thoughts with healing mantras repeatedly. This raised frequency expanded through Ruchi's mind, and her condition improved slightly. The doctors observed this visible change, delaying the unplugging of the life support machines for the next seventy-two hours.

I maintained contact with Ruchi's emotional mind and dream bodies, transmitting a field of thought vibrations to her. A powerful message enveloped her conscious mind. Although the doctors lost hope for recovery, they kept her under strict observation. Sarika called again. I reassured her but also informed her of Ruchi's slow progress in the next two weeks. Meanwhile, each day, I focused on one thought—recovery and regeneration. I continued sending this message to Ruchi through healing mantras.

At the end of two weeks, the nurse observed the slightest movement in Ruchi's toes, but her liver readings showed negligible improvement. I continued tuning into Ruchi's thoughts. Gradually her cells responded, and she recovered.

After three years, Ruchi came to India and visited me with Sarika. 'I remember nothing of the time when I was in a coma. But when I recovered, and thoughts came in, I felt a strange feeling of being wrapped in a wave. This wave grew until it enveloped every part of me. Now when I close my eyes, it does not feel so dark as it did earlier,' she said. Ruchi and her sister Sarika eulogise this intervention and communication of collective thoughts that dart in all directions (with the relativity of time and space). They bear witness to the endless possibilities of connection.

I am also reminded of a treatise I have read on one of the six systems of Indian philosophy—*Vaisesika*. In the book, an Indian physicist Jagdish Bose refers to an article in the scientific journal *East-West*, April 1934. He summarises the ancient text discussing the mobility of *anu* (an atom), the kinetic nature of all energy, and *aakash* (cosmos) as the basis for transmitting subtle forces, vibrations, and frequencies within the relativity of time and space.

This broadly explains the capacity to access a travelling thought if one is aware, focused, and conscious. When a common being breaks away from the continuity of self-oriented thought, she or he enters the threshold of a collective thought. In an interpretation of Aristotle's words, Philosopher Will Durant says, 'We are what we repeatedly do. Excellence then is not an act, but a habit.'

Most people I counsel are unaware of the decades I have spent studying the phenomenon of thoughts. The atmosphere registers every thought and in my heightened awareness, I can hear the echoes of the past, present, and future, all dancing in rhythmic vibrations, revolving around the person in a ripple, a colour, and a form.

Humans take comfort and pride in their identity and sense of belonging. Names, ages, professions, social status, and achievements are the security vests that hold our heads high, shielding us in many ways. Normally, such trivia are the obvious firsts in an introductory meeting of any nature. When in consultation, I deliberately avoid such pleasantries because most people naturally find comfort in self-identity. This attaches an emotion to a voice. Some are indifferent to their name, while others attach a title with pride; some enjoy the sounds in their names and almost sing it poetically, while others shy away from their name or are ashamed of it. So, I begin by asking for the date of birth, writing it on my notepad, therefore making little or no eye contact. This steers the person's mind to a more neutral spot. The day one was born is a done deal. An unchanging, non-negotiable statement. The birth of any creature is its prime connection to the earth. It is the grounding wire. This information enables a neutral stance, giving me undiluted access to the sound vibrations in a voice.

Picture this. There is an unchanging reality—your birth date which mostly remains in the background whereas personal credentials—name, age, country, profession, titles, achievements, disappointments, attachments, judgements, and now the number of Instagram followers—all bubble away at the frontline. When I ask for the date of birth, this mental formation reverses. The tone changes and your voice mirrors the subconscious. This reflects on your personality and blueprint. In the tick-tock of a few seconds, I access every thought travelling in that space. I hear far-reaching echoes in those first whispers and answer the unspoken question.

Ideally, that's it; it's over in two minutes. I have addressed every thought floating in your space. But when I'm done, the never-ending saga begins, and I call out to my staff for a cup of cardamom *chai* for all the guests and me.

With
your name,
each word feels like a story.
A poem,
an ode,
a memoir,
feel mystic in passing.
Just a whisper of my name
on your lips
feels enough
and then every
wave of desire
feels stale in passing.
I am indeed the answer
to your hundred questions
after which,
all desires
feel wearisome in passing.

8

Impressions

'Dr Mishra, even though I am comfortable reciting mantras, my pronunciations are terrible. I am aware it is the tone and accent that make the recital of Sanskrit mantras so musical. The boys tease me constantly and imitate the way I chant a mantra. They say I will never get it because I did not grow up in a Brahmin family. It is so true, and I do not know how to overcome that,' I said, one afternoon at the ashram.

Yogesh Mishra laughed till his stomach hurt. His indifference upset me even more as he lazily stood up from his armchair, stretched and sauntered into the courtyard. He assessed each young man, watching intently, before casually walking back towards me.

'One day Nirmala will be a *mantragya*—the one who embodies the sacred word. She will be a force to reckon with. She will exude the sounds of Sanskrit with a fire from her belly, and you will all shy away from her brilliance. Mark my words,' he said aloud.

Yogesh Mishra repeated the same words for a fortnight, till I finally confronted him, 'Alright now. If I were to believe in your conviction, do also tell me how. What effort do I need to make?'

He sprung to his feet, held my left wrist gently, and guided me to his room. Raising his right palm to settle just above my head, he asked what form of divinity I connected with naturally. When I said Ganesh, he spoke the Ganpati mantra like this, 'Aum gan ganpataye namah'. I repeated the mantra after him. He smiled, and I caught a strange glint in his eye. 'Yes, and now repeat it again. Keep repeating this mantra while you are quiet, while you work, study, play the sitar, or sleep. Chant it even while listening to others. Chant it within you until your breath and the sound of the mantra become one. Repeat this mantra until it turns into an effortless uttering.'

During the nine-day periods, I silently chanted this mantra for hours and sometimes fell into a deep sleep after that. In the beginning, I simply followed instructions, but soon I felt the sounds in my body. I listened to the tone and developed a rhythm as I chanted continuously. But something felt amiss. Like a string of musical notes that did not connect. The sounds blocked my nasal passage. Instead of a steady rhythm in repetition, it felt like a bad composition, with little harmony.

It takes a symphony of word, pitch, rhythm, measure, time, and tempo, to create a verse that one sings repeatedly and effortlessly. A soothing frequency or a feverish excitement that mounts to a crescendo. Sanskrit denotes a refined set of syllables that resonate as perfected verse in rhythm. But I encountered none of the above.

I came to a halt.

After a few deep breaths, I started again, allowing my nose to direct me and soon heard myself chanting, 'Aum *gam* ganpataye namah' instead of 'Aum *gan* ganpataye namah', and my stomach churned twice over. In that moment, 'word' had found its union, its synchronicity, and its *yog*.

I started the repetitions again, often losing sense of time. The more I stayed with the mantra, the more I discovered a distance between the internal and the external. I did not shy away from my day with school, friends, sisters, the daily commute, and the chaos of a busy environment, yet my body and mind longed to repeat the mantra, like a song that lifts you to a resonance, a mood and a high you cannot resist. I felt a strange warmth in the centre of my forehead. A glow. It grew and grew and grew inside and around me. Light and so alive, I felt a renewed vulnerability. I heard the whispers of a butterfly and the roar of faraway clouds. I sat for long hours present in my body yet exposed to something I cannot define. Time became an illusion. Everything receded while I remained alert and conscious of my surroundings.

I wondered if I heard the mantra wrong or Dr Mishra initiated me on an incorrect verse. I do not know because I did not question him. I did not feel the need to. Perhaps it is the difference between teachers and a guru who strips you of your references rather than enforce on you what they have learnt. Dr Mishra purposefully challenged my awareness, intelligence, and creativity. He threw me into the flames and waited to see what I did with the heat. Was I going to follow and recite like a parrot or use the human ability to discern?

He directed me within so I could find the answers for myself. Since then, I have experimented with every mantra I encounter. I allow its frequency the time and space needed to grow within me so I can feel each syllable for tone, melody and scale. I take time to understand what it does to my veins, my bones, my mind, and my heart. I let a mantra percolate till I find the resonance of perfection dancing in my being.

I have no formal learning of the Sanskrit language, but I have mastered the sounds through experiencing the force of a word in silence. I found a personal affinity to each syllable of the language.

A word—the most powerful tool of communication available to a human is paradoxical. It has the power to destroy, manipulate, and influence, yet also enables mass movements if directed with integrity. Such words and speeches exude an exacting energy. They deliver a creative change. Words used with an intense feeling hold the power of sound. The tempo, energy, pace, rhythm, and tone unite to create a shift in the mind, body, and heart of a listener. Thus, a prayer brings hope, and a speech carries a wave of hatred, love, or defiance. Similarly, each mantra has its own purpose. Verses that I have repeated more than a hundred thousand times, are alive, swirling and swaying within me just like the glowing flame of an earthen lamp. They live within me. Steady and vibrant.

So how do I interact with the sounds in a mantra? I understand each mantra much like the seven *swars* (seven musical notes), each representing a different frequency. To accomplish the vibration in any mantra, I focus on the sound of each alphabet. With careful listening and uttering, I understand the tone and pitch of the sound to evaluate its scale—high, medium or low. I follow the tone. The sounds in any mantra engage with a tone, a pitch, and a note. Each syllable uttered fits into one swar or musical note. Therefore, a mantra invokes an effect just as music does on the brain, body, and mind.

Imagine a new harmonium or piano with seven notes. While chanting, I embed certain words into each respective key of this instrument, completing a sequence. When I chant mantras repeatedly, I fit them into their separate purposes and set the tone, pitch, and depth accordingly. The result is penetrating just like a maestro who produces a beautiful piece of music. It is such sounds that lead me to meaning. Meaning leads to a deeper understanding, wisdom and a piercing silence.

With practice, a constructive quality continues to become finer. While one trail of the same sound leads me to an understanding, another trail takes me to an experience. I say this because it is what my days, nights and all the moments in between are about. I breathe, knead, knit, think, and chant these mantras constantly within me, like a song playing in the background. When I chant for someone, the thought travels through a concentrated tunnel of frequency and heals. It affects the other while leaving another mark on me too. Each time I chant, the technique and process become sharper. Just like a classical dancer who can still dance as light as a feather at the age of eighty. The dancer becomes one with the dance. Similarly, a chant dives deeper and deeper within me, and I feel lighter in it.

Chanting mantras is now an effortless act. What began at thirteen is still growing within me in the present. In all the darkness of illusions, I feel bright and fearless. I visualise the sharp, blinding intensity of colour and its subtlety. Each word I chant reverberates as a distant whisper, an echo, and a rainbow within me.

The brightest form of a sunrise and sunset is golden. It reflects the other hues in its intensity, signalling light from a sun, millions of miles beyond the earth. The frequency of sound belongs somewhere in that field of light in the known universe. Similarly, the highest vibrations in a mantra travel far into the expanses of the universe and reverberate back as a bright golden hue above my head. And I experience a tangible connection to each ray of the golden sun.

In retrospect, Dr Mishra nurtured a dormant seed within me. He nudged it, coaxed it, and watered it till it cracked open to sprout, after which he enabled it to explore freely, without premeditated conditions, references or boundaries. And now when I meet a young person, I often notice a new life in the near future. It brings me immense pleasure to nudge, hint, guide, and push people out of their comfort zones to think creatively. Any event, whether sad or joyous, induces powerful emotions. This is where an opportunity emerges and a seed sprouts. It holds the probability of expansion. But a human mind often wavers. One must pause and ask a question: 'Do I have the courage to follow the rumbling of a new beginning? Can I follow a creative purpose, walk into the unknown, or will I remain loyal to familiarity?'

Dr Mishra walked me to the treasure maps I needed. He did not suppress my stubbornness but channelled it so I could carry the creativity in a single thought to its culmination. He explained every hidden concept considering my age, my abilities and my capacity. When I tired of his analytical approaches, he steered me to one more ancient tale, and one more myth. Parables are strange creatures; each time you pay them a visit, they unearth just a little more.

A sage lived in the mountains with a group of seekers. One day, a student, missing for months, suddenly reappeared. When the sage questioned his long absence, this student pulled out a thin glass bottle bubbling with a mixture of green chemicals, saying he had found the perfect formula for turning most things into gold.

The sage jumped up, snatched the bottle from the student, unscrewed the lid open, and poured the contents on a small mound nearby. Now, the little knoll of mud turned into pure gold. The student first jumped in delight at his achievement and then threw a fit, criticising the sage for pouring out the whole concoction.

The master yelled back at him, saying, 'You spent months running after these chemicals. Great! But you did not change one bit; your anger, greed, and arrogance remain untouched by the glittering gold you created. If you had stated your wish right in the beginning, I would have sorted it so we could get on with more important matters.'

This student shouted back, 'Since you are a master, I assume you can achieve anything,' and saying so, he chose a big hill in the area, challenging the sage. 'Well, let us see you turn that hill into gold to prove your ability, master.'

The sage walked up the hill and had a leisurely pee at the very top, while the student saw it whirling into threads of gold.

The master turned to face the stunned boy and said, 'All minerals and chemicals in nature are part of a body too. The forces of the universe make up the framework of a common being. You searched outside of the self and produced one bottle of minerals, which changed a mound of mud to gold. As a result, you discovered a renewed sense of your individual worth but did nothing to know yourself better. If you wish to achieve genuine change and find your creativity, turn inwards my friend, and you will find much more than the false glitter of a metal. You will find gold. Gold that shines fearlessly with purpose in the progress of a collective humanity.'

This story stayed with me. I was never sure of where the words landed, but they surely impressed upon me. Seeds of wisdom lie dormant within us all. When we hunt down our deepest intentions with brutal honesty, a renewed humility cracks these seeds, nudging us back to a more conscious life, away from the complexities of a corrupt mind.

In his later years, Yogesh Mishra chose to live far away from the pressures of a conditioned society. I have not seen him in three decades but feel a rare connection to him, as alive as when I was thirteen. He rarely spoke of his guru but often said, 'When one's guru emanates a brilliance, the student does not beg for her or his own existence. One does not need to. Wherever one stands, growth manifests itself through the radiance of the guru, expanding and evolving as far as the other end of the universes.'

I rarely speak of my guru or the method in mantra. It is personal, just like the *mala* which is primarily used for chanting. Intimate, special, and never on display. Beyond borders, common beings have used strings of beads for prayer, ritual, discipline, hope, security and as a coping mechanism. Is there any value in such objects?

I often find that a question may contain the answer too. A common being constantly looks for relative value in form, clinging on to an anchor when in doubt. So, there is relative value in everything till it serves its purpose.

Personally, a mala (made of seeds) is a reminder of the whole. When I use a mala, I am conscious of an entirety, a completion, or a cycle in a seed. A seed reminds me of the wholeness of a mother. She kindles, rekindles and realigns my breath with the breath of this precious earth. In essence, mala is a high-frequency Sanskrit word, wherein 'ma' denotes the mother and 'la' comes from the word *lau* (a flame). Strung together, a mala symbolises the creative consciousness that we are, constantly evolving as a race, thriving, flowing into an unknown future with hope, faith, awareness and a search for the elusive self.

When thoughts of you scatter
in these spaces around me,
a new dawn arrives on its own.
I visit a shrine,
I tie a wish fulfilling thread,
I see it smiling in your name.
And
what do I say of your memory?
Memories of you
are like a lamp in a shrine
If the lamp burns out…
people come
and light it again.

9

Back to the Beginning

'Nirmala, the postman came this morning with a letter addressed to you. I kept it on the centre table in the living room. I wonder what it is about?' Maa said when I came back from college one afternoon in March 1982, just two weeks after my 18th birthday. I carefully opened the sealed envelope while having tea. It was an official invite from the Benares Hindu University, Varanasi, to take part in a scholars' conference on Indian astrology, occult, and Vedic sciences.

What a beautiful surprise it was. The opportunity delighted me. Later that evening, after dinner, I tiptoed nervously into my father's study. I paused for a moment outside his door, looked at the letter again, and wondered, 'Will he say yes or no? I know there's little scope for any excesses after all the monthly expenses he has.'

'Nirmala, I will think about it,' he had said.

Three days later, I was with Maa in the kitchen when father came in and stood close behind me, waving two air tickets in my face. I snatched them out of his hands as he dodged me.

'Oh my God! Does this mean we will fly to Varanasi, daddy?' I said hugging him. Excited, I packed a little bag while Maa said I should look mature enough to be among scholars. We chose a handwoven, forest green, *kota zari* sari, with a luxurious ruby-red and gold border. I tied my hair in a single long braid and wore wedged heels for that perfect bounce.

It felt exciting yet nerve-wracking. Daddy laughed as I clapped at intervals, like a little child on a new adventure. This was my first plane journey. Taking the window seat, I clutched my daddy's right hand and chanted mantras till we touched ground in Varanasi. As I cautiously stepped off the airstair, I looked back to see the plane for a good minute. I smiled, knowingly. I was not dreaming.

Standing outside the arrival gates, I inhaled deeply, just to feel the air. I was in one of the world's most ancient cities—Kashi or the one that shines eternally. There are fewer places on earth of greater antiquity and none other with an uninterrupted continuity of its history, culture, and spiritual distinction. In that moment, I remembered the famous lines of American author, Mark Twain, who wrote, 'Benares is older than history, older than tradition, even older than legend, and looks twice as old as all of them put together.'

Daddy hailed a taxi straight to the venue. We showed the letter at the main entrances of the sprawling university and the guard directed the driver to a red stone building that housed the faculty of Sanskrit. Walking down the large descending central hall was like a stroll through history—large ceiling fans whirring overhead in slow motion, the light seeping in through wooden framed arched windows, and walls standing high and mighty in the play of light and shadows. I stood mesmerised for a moment at the entrance. My eyes scanned the auditorium, starting from my right to the far left, and all the way down. I saw most seats taken by male scholars and a few young men standing around too, but my eyes searched for one woman, my age… or any age. An escort soon showed us to our seats in the third row from the front. He mentioned the names of a few women scholars invited. This was the second day of a four-day conference, and I was the only woman in the gallery.

Soon, the loud chattering turned to a quiet murmur, and a convenor addressed the gathering, introducing the guest speakers. Half an hour later, as is the tradition, he put forward the question of the day as a starting point for an open debate. 'If four children are born in the same country, within identical planetary combinations, time, and date, how do each of them have diverse tendencies, behaviours, and predicaments?'

There was a nervous shuffling in the hall as a senior professor came on stage for the introductory talk. I felt the annoying loud pitch of the microphone. Alert and stiff, I also sensed a wave of energy within me, anxiously waiting for its release. I listened attentively to each point and argument made by visiting lecturers, and raised my hand several times to speak, soon realising the futility of it. I was no professor and the students in the hall did not raise their hands. Each time I looked at my father for support, he gestured for me to be patient and wait for my turn.

At one point, I looked at my watch and realised it was three hours since they put the question forward. Soon they would break up for tea. Another forty-five minutes passed, and I raised my hand several more times, observing that the discussion had now taken off on a tangent. I wanted to stand up and scream, 'We are missing the point here.'

In that frustrated moment, I stood up, marched straight down the aisle and climbed the three steps to the stage. Then I waited at the edge for the speaker (a professor) to finish his sentence. As soon as he did, I rushed to where he stood, clutched the long arm of the microphone stand, and just waited. It confused the tall, dhoti-clad, silver-haired man, and he turned to look at me through his round, rimmed glasses. I looked back at him, straight in the eye.

With palpable anger, he glared at me threateningly and shouted, 'Behave little girl! Mind yourself before you speak, as the brains of a young girl like you, lie tied in that long braid.' Without any response, I grabbed the mike off the stand and ran to the other end of the stage, for safe distance. I straightened up, almost marking my space before I spoke to the speaker, 'I apologise for an impolite entry, yet strongly believe the discussion has strayed from the subject.' He stepped back against the black panels of the stage, while I turned to face the audience.

'Friends,' I said, clearing my throat, 'as we are aware, the accuracy of astrological theories depends on precise principles. Planetary movements and mathematical calculations do not falter, but a human sometimes stumbles, thus falling short in the inferences. A multitude of geographies, environments, histories, cultures, and traditions enable the channelling of knowledge into different schools of thought. Within this framework, I wish to present my analysis on the question of identical birth time versus differing human behaviours.'

After all these years, I can still sense the frozen atmosphere in the room. Strangely, no one stepped forward to reprimand me. I took a deep breath before I continued, 'As astrologers, we make life charts based on the date of birth and time which may be the same for person a, b and c, yet the chart shows different destinies. Why? This is because we cannot know a clear date of conception. The journey of a sperm to an embryo is unique to each one. It can be one day, three days, a week, or even more, therefore the ambiguity. Pregnancy begins once the fertilised egg implants in the uterus, and then it takes roughly ten weeks for the embryo to develop into a body that breathes independently of the mother. It is at this precise moment, when the new body breathes on its own, that the stars, the moon, and the rays of the sun affect its growth in a womb. This moment again is unique to each one. Astrologers do not begin calculations at this point. We simply cannot. All planetary calculations begin from the recorded time at birth and not when the conceived baby breathes separately in the womb of its mother. And as each human is deeply influenced by the planets this variation is one of the reasons for the diverse lives and behaviours of children/people born at an identical time.'

I paused, clutching the microphone tighter with both hands, before I spoke again, 'Secondly, no baby is born in 287 days; some birth between 38 to 40 weeks, and some before 37 weeks. This also affects a baby's alignment with the position of stars which results in gaps during calculations. If I take this point a step further, we can then confirm why some twins have contrasting personalities, interests, and dilemmas in life. Thirdly, cultural backgrounds, class, religious structure, and geographical environments play a large part in a person's behaviour patterns. All these reasons account for the diverse predicaments of those born at an identical time on earth. Thank you.'

I finally let go of my tight grip over the microphone stand, taking a step backwards. My eyes hovered around the hall. I heard some claps and murmurs. After a minute, a few professors in the front row thumped their desks. One of them stood up and asked, 'How can you know this at your age? It is commendable.'

I folded my hands and replied, '*Hukum*, apart from observing the world through maun, I have also studied the *Mansagari* and *Laghu Parashri*, among other texts and publications.'

'Well done,' he said.

Then I heard myself speak the next few lines: 'And Hukum, because I am a young girl with my brains stuck in my long braid, possibly this important piece of information nestled in there, and I could access it when needed. However, men generally have slack hair, never tied down in braids, so the much-needed evidence slips through their unruly ends!'

That was it. Silence followed the abrupt laughter of cynics. I walked straight back to where my father was and slowly turned to look at him. He sat so still one might mistake him for a statue. In that lingering silence, I understood the inconsistency between a thought, idea, spoken words, and actual performance. Was I invited just to tick a box? Female student invited. Checked and confirmed.

That afternoon a high wall in that building lay split down the middle. I heard the first cracks struggling to accept a young woman as an equal. With the second cracks came the loud sounds of inappropriate male pride that deliberately ignored a woman's request for a voice. I also heard the eerie silence of a father's dilemma caught between cultural convention and his daughter's right to the freedom of expression.

Stepping out of the dark hallways, I stood at the threshold of a long struggle. Although I did not regret my forced intervention or my words, it left me with little choice but to walk alone in the corridors of a Hindu Brahmin's privileged inheritance. I never received further invitations from Vedic interventions of any kind. Since then, I refuse to acknowledge or accept the imposed higher position of a patriarchal body.

Despite it being a traditionally partisan institution, I have never played the victim, nor do I shout about my disadvantage as a woman. It defeats the purpose because in most societies, a man and a woman both endure struggles while learning skills. I apply the same discipline and focus and thus my work speaks for me. When critics, reviewers, or colleagues protest, it is partly because they fear another's worth. Criticism mostly originates from deep-rooted insecurities and a lack of self-worth.

I believe a constructive, creative thought expands limitlessly. It vibrates. It multiplies and reverberates. I may pen a poem in an intuitive, soft moment, but it is the way one recites or narrates it that creates a vibration. A voice, a sound and a resounding echo. This vibration carries forward and touches another. Creativity shows its face—neutral and indivisible It blossoms . . . unbound, unbroken, and independent in the face of a divided world.

❧

If you must take,
take a step forward,
there will always be those who pull you back.
If you must dream,
dream high,
there will always be those who look down on you.
If you must,
then provoke sparks of passion
within you
there will always be those who fuel envy.
If you must create
create your plan, create your destiny,
there will always be those who idle in gossip.
If you must love,
love yourself,
love your divinity,
there will always be those who incite hostility.

10

Jigsaw Puzzles

It was the peak of summer in 1986 when I met a lady from the royalty of Rajasthan. She was a woman in her early forties, grappling with depression and sadness at her inability to bear a child.

'I feel incomplete as a woman and fear that my sister-in-law's six children will be heirs to the royal clan,' she said.

'So how can I help you?' I asked her.

'The doctors confirm I can still conceive. There is no abnormality in the womb. But I am doubtful, anxious and have little hope. I have heard of your insight and abilities as a siddha mantragya. I am hoping you can heal me so I may hold a baby in my arms.'

'Look, I am young, at an experimental stage and cannot risk interfering with the anatomy. I cannot help you,' I said. But this woman persuaded me like none other. She had firmly decided I could deliver her wish. I was young and naive, with little understanding of the ways of the mind. I gave in, hoping it might stop the constant pleading.

I thought of how I could invoke a shift in the woman's body and researched how subtle knowledge could be used to rearrange imbalances within a body to revive a possibility pre-existent in the womb. For the next fortnight, I studied the efficacy of tantra and occult, applying formulas to rearrange aspects which may have fallen out of place, much like a piece that needs to fit correctly in a jigsaw puzzle.

A month later, I performed a penetrating fire ceremony with the woman. A three-hour-long yagya efficiently coordinated within the organised movement of light, sound, pace, energy, and ratio; five aspects pre-existent within the constant movement of our universe—the *mahayagya*. This was a micro ceremony mirroring the macro in a discreet alliance; the consummation of a small fire into a cosmic fire, and an individual womb with the primordial womb.

I was a busy twenty-one-year-old in the last year of undergraduate study and almost forgot about this ceremony till one night I had a dream. Standing alone in a meadow at twilight, I saw a lady come from the distance. She stopped a few feet away. I strained my ears to hear her saying, 'I will conceive within eighteen months.'

I smiled on waking early the next morning and when the woman came to meet me again, I casually told her of my dream. The news delighted her.

Two years later at a relative's wedding, a member of the royal family arrived unannounced and asked for me. I walked to the central hall and saw the same woman running towards me. With tears running down her cheeks, she bent down to lay a baby at my feet. Embarrassed, I picked up the child, stared at the overwhelmed mother with questioning eyes, and thought, 'Well, good for her! She has adopted a baby. Thankfully, common sense prevailed.'

'Thank you for your help, Nirmala. This is my firstborn,' she said.

Her words shocked me. The fire ceremony, the mantras and my dream—all the scenes flooded back. I quietly acknowledged the baby in my arms. This woman had no treatment from doctors. So, what happened? Obviously, various aspects such as energy, sound, and the elements affected the healing process and brought about a shift within the woman's body and mind, arousing an existing possibility. Energy is neither created nor destroyed. It is the proportionate ratio of light, sound, pace, and energy that undergoes a change. Therefore, through this alchemy, a tantric yagya expert attracts a field of frequencies, easing the correction and subsequent growth of a dormant energy.

Sound waves transcend destruction. They remain in our universe as a floating vibration. The application of sound (frequencies in a mantra) and fire (elements) in a precise combination, enables a field of concentrated energy in the environment. This is broadly how a mantra combined with a fire ceremony works for an occultist. When I chant during a fire ceremony, I repeat a certain mantra, focussing on the purpose. After a while, I ask the participants to concentrate deeper on the situation or the desire. This is a state of concentration—*kumbhak avastha*.

Fire also cleans up the immediate environment. A yagya ceremony involves the use of fragrant sandalwood, various herbs, and roots, all-natural purifiers that burn the heavy, gross aspects in a person or the environment to access the lighter, more refined qualities present in the atmosphere. A fire ceremony for general purposes differs from healing yagyas performed with a more specific purpose, to alter the sounds, frequency, and energy. The ingredients and other elements differ too, just like a medicine designed specifically for an ailment.

Ritual in any form has its special formation. The preparation is a deliberate process, a contemplation, almost like half a prayer said, and half a dream shared. I take special care and attention to detail while applying certain formulas during healing yagyas. I like to call these my recipes. For instance, contrary to using the more popular cow dung, I use *javitri*, *jaiphul, jau,* and *chandan* powder as healing ingredients for a Gayatri yagya ceremony. For a Sri yagya, I start with a dry coconut in the *kund* and then white and red sandalwood, after which I offer thirty-six healing ingredients and seven fragrances: chandan, *khas,* champa, lotus, amber, *kesar,* and *harshringhar.* For the relief of pain and suffering, a Maha Mritunjaya yagya involves using three cooling fragrances: mogra, *chameli,* champa, and another sixteen healing ingredients or *aushadhi.*

For a *Vashikaran* yagya, a ceremony to influence desires, I use white musk perfume, night jasmine, and white sandalwood. For a *Prabhavvriddhi* yagya, a ceremony to extract the attraction available in one's environment, an occultist uses products with strong magnetic properties. I use powerful fragrances for enticing the other; frangipani, white musk, sandalwood, *rajnigandha,* and lotus along with healing ingredients such as *agar, tagar, guggal, shetavri,* and *gokhru.* A common attraction between the male and female culminates into the natural step of conception. To turn this conception into a seed, I perform a particular ceremony with *kleem* mantras—the seeds of attraction.

There is a purpose behind each yagya. It is a ceremony with the elements, to the elements, and for the elements. A yagya functions just like a refinery; an installation that refines matter to a new purity. The purity of an elemental body promotes clarity in both the mind and the core. To further refine the core, a practitioner must recede within, to the centre.

I remember the incident of the newborn for several reasons. It made me more cautious and sceptical of what people asked of me. I started listening more to the silence, to the unspoken words hovering around a person. I observed clients for longer, studying the shift in their bodies, the steadiness in their eyes, and the movement of their hands while they spoke. I also began the long and constant process of paying more attention to my feelings, thoughts, and intuition, trusting none other than myself and the voice within.

This event was a revelation on the manipulations of the mind. I remember the woman's sister-in-law had called me too, telling me I was wasting my time with an older woman. She had said, 'How many older women do you know that deliver a baby at forty-five?' The truth is I did not. I realised my ignorance in areas outside of metaphysical research. Like a frog in my little pond, I did not interact more than my areas of interest. I just did not care. I began the process of re-discovery, reading diverse authors and their philosophies, while appreciating different interactions and stories of the world I live in.

Yet the moment felt surreal when I held the baby in my arms. A deep vulnerability touched each person in the room—an awkward feeling hard to rationalise. This is why my sisters remember it so clearly. Somewhere they found more confidence in me, in a powerful yet subtle life force and the hidden potential of creativity. I bow to an unknown superior consciousness. It bewilders me. I realise I am an instrument to something much more profound.

This experience renewed my sense of responsibility with the work I do. Somewhere I had turned a corner to understand the finer aspects of occult methods. I also discovered the false attitude and narratives towards such practices. The words tantra or occult conjure up a dramatized gory version. People cling to old perspectives and superstitions filled with fear rather than trying to understand better. In contrast, I learnt that the Yajur Ved was originally not part of a religion one could claim. It is not spiritualism either but a well-demonstrated treatise of pristine cryptic knowledge, or *gyan*, efficiently accessible through persistent effort and study like many other fields of knowledge.

Imagine a person suffering from chronic back pain. I conduct a fire ceremony with two healing mantras for the alleviation of the suffering. Chanting with the correct intonation results in the continuous collision of vibrations and the repetition generates a higher frequency field. The charged energy field thus aids in the realigning process of the mind and the body, allowing the healing process. Yet, in this intangible process, it is the person's intent that keeps the doors and windows open for the desired change to happen. As humans, we thrive in our constant hope for the better. This tenacious hold on hope also creates a placebo effect, allowing the necessary room for change.

Soon, I had people seeking me out for familial dilemmas, financial stability, to save a terminally ill child or a parent. People also made appointments for supplementary relief of chronic pains, depression, and some for the abnormal behaviours in their children. A year after the last experiment, I encountered another unforgettable situation while performing an environment cleansing *Shudhi* yagya. This was a fire ceremony with mantras for an affluent family living at the Bagru haveli in a town of the same name, thirty-five kilometres away from Jaipur. After the ceremony, the mother anxiously spoke of her twelve-year-old boy's odd behaviour. I assessed he had mental health problems and recommended a visit to the psychiatrist. But the lady insisted I suggest a remedy. I said she could try stone therapy; a ruby to reduce the effects of the disturbing planets in his charts.

There were slight improvements, but his behaviour remained erratic. He did not eat well, had terrible mood swings, cried inconsolably, had trouble focusing on tasks, and sometimes just sat for long hours, staring with blank eyes. The following week the family visited our home in Jyoti Nagar and spoke at length about the boy's condition. They thought there was something untoward bothering the child. I did not believe in the paranormal but once again gave in to their request and agreed to perform a fire ceremony with the specific purpose of cleaning the boy's environment. I reasoned that while a fire burns, it purifies anything in its way.

About forty women and men assembled on the terraced first floor of the old palace. I deliberately sat facing a bare white wall on the west side of the terrace, while the boy and his parents sat to my left and the grandparents to the right. All the others sat behind the two parties. The boy's mother helped me set up the ritual. I arranged the *havan kund* in the centre—a semi-circular large clay vessel to burn a fire. In this large bowl, I placed a few sandalwood sticks, a dry coconut, cardamoms, bay leaf, cloves, and other aromatics. We arranged four platters of fresh flowers in three colours: white jasmine, red roses, and orange marigolds. The lady also laid out small plates with various dried herbal roots and leaves as offerings into the fire for all the family taking part in the ceremony. I lit the fire with a piece of camphor.

I poured ghee into the clay dish and watched the hard outer shell of the coconut crack in surrender to the rising flames. A wild combination of fragrances danced sensuously to the left and right of my nostrils. I took a deep breath, closed my eyes, retreated inwards and began chanting. The family placed the offerings into the fired-up clay pot at regular intervals and the flames rose. I used a long wooden ladle to pour more ghee, exciting the flames enough to dance higher. The audience receded while I accessed subtle sounds reverberating in symphony with the heartbeat. I was in it.

Thirty-five minutes into the ritual, I went deeper into praying for rejuvenation of the boy's energies and directed the parents to visualise themselves in white while I placed white jasmine flowers in their palms. Just then, I saw four naked children, seven to nine years old, appear abruptly on the bare white wall in front of me. There were no children in the room when I started, so I performed all the mental checks, blinked, and looked again. These children sat staring with blank eyes. I blinked again. I surely did not see any naked children on my way into the haveli. Who were they and how did they get there?

I looked behind the three rows of people. The white walls of the terrace were bare. Then I looked at the wall in front of me again. These naked children continued zooming in and out of my vision. I looked down and then looked up again. They were there; adolescent boys sitting on the walls with their bare legs hanging down. Just there. Not much movement.

I sat cross-legged with about forty pairs of eyes watching me. An icy shiver ran through my spine, and I felt it right down to the coccyx. Standing almost too swiftly, I ran down the flight of steps to the courtyard. Out of the forty-odd people, twenty-five of them confirmed they saw the four children too. I was sweating, panting, and shaking my head, while refusing to go back to complete the ceremony. The elders were still up there, and one person came down to calm my nerves. After much placation, insistence and three glasses of cold water, I agreed and finished the yagya, making peace with the so-called wanderers.

The parents called our house in a month informing us that the boy's behaviour was gradually changing, and he took more interest in his daily life. The father had researched the history of the palace and said the story went back fifty years ago when two noble people lived there with their families. A feud with another clan in the palace killed their four young children. The brutal deaths resulted in these traumatised, tormented, and frightened beings, and this heavy fear hovered in the corners of that big house, eventually manifesting in the boy.

For a long while after this incident, I did not step out much. I remember constantly watching my back, looking to see if someone stood behind me. The thought of being under the surveillance of elusive beings frightens me. But it got me thinking although I am still sceptical of it. Where the ruby failed, the fire did the job.

I contemplated the efficacy of occult practices. All creatures are a spark of light. When light does not pass from one body to another, a few sparks hit off as remnants. A body dies, but the thoughts in an individual mind exist on this earth, ever present in the atmosphere. Thoughts of fear, anger, lust, and deep jealousy make the air heavy. And because the thought or the tendency exists, it manifests in the vulnerable.

Was it the extreme trauma of those children coming through? Or was it the intense fear lurking in the palace that touched the boy? And what made the naked children appear? I realised I did not attract something of the earth but something outside of it or below it. This happened at the start of my research when I was more open to adventure, and any bit of information excited me. I wanted to witness possibilities, to re-imagine the so-called boundaries, evaluate theories for myself rather than believe another's story, and so I went all the way to reach the goalpost. With no belief in the paranormal/ghost theory, I did not expect results, let alone seeing what I did. After reading a small text on *Pret vidya* (paranormal study), I assessed the experiment with little research. I used bones, a skull, ashes, and other such objects which an associate, Prem bhai found on my insistence. He got them from a professor who practised tantra in Jawahar Nagar. Later, I even wondered why these people helped me.

This experience opened my mind to worlds that exist beyond the normal perceptions of the human mind. If or when rebirth happens, the life force within travels from one causal body to the next. The time in between is crucial, because it is during this period that the vulnerable may stray. Interestingly, these spirits that I saw were the same age as when they died. Therefore, rebirth did not occur. If I consider the theory that matter remains the same but form changes; here, in all probability, the form did not change. It remained stuck. This is a subjective study into the possibilities of brutal, abnormal, and accidental deaths. Personally, I stayed away from the paranormal. But I also realised that the subtle worlds exist, and this introduced me to the existing diversity of ideas and theories.

Hundreds of experiments have helped me weave a tiny corner of an immense picture—the extreme potential of conscious thought, intuition, and limitless awareness. I am still learning the interdependency between galaxies, this universe, the stars, earth, the rivers, and the human body.

I do not own titles or a hierarchical surname, yet in the last four decades, I have experimented on sixty-seven combinations of fire ceremonies and sounds to realign a human's micro limitations with the unlimited capacities of the macro—the universe. All with the purpose of fostering an evolution; a collective well-being and a spirited humanity.

Your love . . .
a drop of morning dew
resting on the tip of a leaf.
Your love . . .
the seven mystic hues
of a rainbow.
Your love . . .
the untouched fragrance
of a jasmine flower.
Your love
the burning lamp
in a silver paten.

Your love . . .
a wish fulfilling talisman
on a saint's crypt.
And my love?
That deep red sun
searching for its identity in the ocean.

11

Arrows in Flight

In the early eighties, while I was at university, my precious little bubble was colourful, over-confident, and invincible. My mother, siblings, extended family, and people who came seeking answers mostly took my word, prediction, judgement, and decisions without a question.

In 1985, I studied Sociology at Kanoria College, Jaipur. Involved with theatre, music, and a vibrant group of young people, I stepped into a new world brimming with ideas, opportunities, and distractions. I idolised our college counsellor, Ms Reeta Mathur. Graceful is the word that best describes her. Each morning, walking past her in the corridors, my shoulders, back, and neck straightened up on impulse. I sensed her joy in wearing exquisitely woven cotton saris; like she was serenading the artist who sat there weaving those colourful threads into a six-yard magnificence. Her presence exuded a sense of ownership. She belonged to herself, and I was in awe.

I watched Ms Reeta Mathur and copied her stride; short steady steps showing her heels but never disturbing the pleats of her sari. Her hair rested on the nape in a neat low bun and sleeveless blouses confidently revealed her slender arms. I imbibed her femininity, her confidence, her dignity, and her style. I took extra care of appearance and this elegance showed in my theatre performances as well. I played various historical roles, portraying a woman in her many personas, as a mother, a warrior, an artist, and a daughter; all with a sense of pride in who I wished to define as an independent woman.

There was one time when I fought for the role I wanted. The director thought I was too short, coaxing me to play the mother's role, but I was far too stubborn and argued till he saw sense in me playing the rebellious daughter instead. I loved theatre and developed a wide-ranging repertoire of roles during that phase. I imagined I was more popular as a theatre artist, but people were far more inquisitive about my unique disposition even though I stayed discreet about it as much as possible.

One day, after a lecture in the afternoon, a senior professor of Hindi, Ms Sharan, asked me for an insight into her future. After a little persuasion, I obliged, blurting that her husband may have cardiac problems in the next five months. As fate would have it, the man suffered a heart attack in July, two months before the five months were up. It forced the professor to go on a long leave from work. At the end of October, she returned to the university. We were in the middle of a lecture when Ms Sharan stormed into the classroom and stood near the lecturer. I noticed her head jogging sharply from the left to the right as she scanned the room till our eyes met.

In the following moments, I felt the sting of a sharp slap across my right cheek. A few students stood up, while others let out a synchronised gasp. The professor stood too close for comfort and our eyes locked in an intense gaze.

'Nirmala Sewani, many can predict events and happenings, but I challenge you to use your intelligence in saving a life. Find a remedy or say a few kind words. Or perhaps when you foresee strong predicaments, keep quiet rather than trigger unnecessary havoc. That would help,' she said.

I stood there with my mouth wide open, searching for the right words while she turned around and walked straight out of the door. No one had ever dared or challenged me in such a way. My pride hit a high ceiling, bounced off the four walls, and dropped hard on the cemented tiles, shattering into a million pieces. I visibly shivered as I heard a piercing echo run down my spine in the most unbearable pitch and tone.

That night I tossed and turned in bed, imagining myself in a wife's role, the one living in constant fear of losing her husband. I felt her extreme paranoia, her fear for the worst, and the related projection of the inevitable. The information of an impending danger had influenced her thoughts and freaked her out. She lost control and, in the process, her worst nightmare manifested at great speed.

The next morning, I sensed a deep change, like I had abandoned my precious bubble during the night. I had shed a cloak and now had nowhere to hide. The past felt playful, but it did not exist anymore. The ground shifted and I did not know where or how to start again. So, I took a deep breath and first accepted where I was. Sitting at the breakfast table, I picked at my food. The day involuntarily started with feedback from my father. We spoke at length, examining the impact of my words on siblings, friends, and clients. I realised the perils of hasty speech, of speaking from where I stood steadfast, consumed with my belief rather than walking the distance to where the other was. The distance between me and you, the distance between a parent and a child, between a man and a woman, between a grandparent and a teenager, between an employer and the employee, between a mother and a daughter-in-law, and between hearing and listening. This distance defines our different worlds. I decided to come unstuck, to become adaptable, to shift and walk this gap and to use my abilities to enter another person's world, closing in on the distance.

I am the oldest of my five siblings. My sisters always relied on me for most decisions, from the colours of their dresses to career choices. Geeta, like the other three sisters, believed what I said without a question. She reasoned and justified her confidence with a question, 'Why wouldn't I trust what you say, Nirmala? Your intuition is spot on with everyone. I cannot deny the accuracy. I am your sister.'

As we grew up into young women, one evening we spoke of men, marriage, and partners. I prophesied on appearances and characters of their future relationships, casually warning Geeta of constant communication problems with her intimate partner. For Geeta, these words lived and breathed in the most sensitive layer of her body: the skin. They resurfaced each time she encountered a conflict with her husband. In one emotionally charged moment, Geeta said, 'Your words do not go away Nirmala. They hang like a sword waiting to slice my sanity.'

I did not sleep for many nights after my sister's outburst. Every waking hour, I scrutinised the seriousness of my predicament. Forced to look into previously unknown layers, I stood face to face with the damage of both irresponsible timing and words. I pictured a spoken word just like an arrow in flight. The responsibility of the archer lies in releasing the bow-string with a pre-meditated force. This intensity pushes an arrow to a desired destination. Similarly, depending on the pace and tone, a released word carries weight. A word holds the potential to poison, to kill, to care, to heal, to influence, or to inspire. When words carelessly slip and land with a thud, we say, 'Sorry, I didn't mean that' or 'it is not the way you understood what I said.' The mind rushes to defend itself. It finds an effortless, careless resistance and figures a way to twist it all in order to wiggle out, and that is it; it is over.

Just as the earth absorbs all of what we give it—manure, fertilisers, plastic bottles, carbon emissions and such—so do we as humans. The human body responds to thoughts and words through pores, nerves, the bloodstream, brain cells, bones, the stomach, and the subconscious mind. The effect is colossal. It leads to clarity, kindness, humility, and patience or fear, disease, and schizophrenia. Decades later, I am glad Geeta found relief in knowing I have learnt along the way. I now question the validity of truth in the larger well-being of a person.

Standing at crossroads after the professor's incident, I had serious choices to make: Which way did I want to go? I retreated to find answers in the expanses of silence. While reading journals, both spiritual and scientific, I contemplated the same concept for months. Nothing in creation creates or destroys at will. A universal law. I observed a repetitive cycle of birth, growth, and decay, and growth again—a continuous, unaltered pattern. So, nothing in the sequence claims a new creation midway. Death and renewal are inevitable. A wave in the ocean hits its end eventually. All we can do is put up barriers and precautions to lessen the impact of the crashing wave. So, where could I find these barriers? I looked into every nook and corner for more than what I already knew and had experimented with.

One day I got a little booklet as a gift. This little handbook had a list of precious stones and gems with pictures and charts that showed their natural properties. Ghanshyam Wadhwa, a precious gems specialist, had compiled basic information on how to examine the quality of a stone and its properties. I touched on the subject, intrigued but sceptical. History shows that it was commonplace in the indigenous, Indian, and Arab worlds to wear precious and semi-precious stones to relieve oneself of heavier influences. But I was looking for a more plausible explanation.

I studied the origin and nature of the nine precious gems: diamond, ruby, emerald, blue sapphire, yellow sapphire, pearl, coral, hessonite garnet, and cat's eye. I understood that precious gemstones are the most organised, stable examples of physical matter in the natural world. I dived into another book, *Ratna Pradip*, by Dr Gauri Shankar Kapur, that covered the advanced study of gems. It detailed the connection between the properties of a certain gem to its corresponding colour, planet, and star in the cosmos. In a gradual process deep in the earth, crystals, hard pressed with one another, fossilise, metamorphosing into different minerals and rocks, eventually forming precious gems. I concluded that just as a body made up of five elements functions and performs within a specific energy field, similarly, metamorphic rocks reverberate with relative energy patterns.

Transparent appearances and the intense colours of gems like emeralds, sapphires, and rubies exude a brilliance, a life force visible under the telescopic view, resembling thin rays of rainbows seen through any crystal on a sunny morning. Each crystal or gemstone when viewed through a prism becomes visible in its wavelength and emits a specific cosmic colour ray. This energised colour ray corresponds with the identical wavelength of a star, gaining a specific vibrancy which any person wearing a gem may absorb.

Gems influence healing processes because of the effect of coloured rays that fall onto a gem through the sphere of its corresponding star: the sun, Mercury, Saturn, Jupiter, Venus, Mars, and the Moon. I studied the relationship between precious gems, colour rays emitted from stars, and a person's birth chart. The specific distance of a planet from the earth and the rays emitted from that planet to the earth into a specific body, at a specific angle, collectively determine the prescription of a gemstone for healing a certain ailment or situation.

When I pestered Prakash Surana, a jeweller in Jaipur, to help me understand the clarity and transparency of a gem, he referred me to his engineers. For months, I assessed various precious gems for quality, size, cutting, grinding, and polishing. I learnt about angles and edges, all created with precision and care at a lapidary. These features contribute to the quality and healing properties of a gem. Sharp angles emit a ray of colour and attract the corresponding ray of colour in a star. The alchemy produces a filtered ray at a particular angle, determining the quality of a gem. Wearing this gem (exposing it from the back of a bespoke ornament) allows the emission of filtered rays for a limited time. The body thus absorbs a colour ray to compensate for a deficiency. We know it takes eight minutes for the rays of the sun to touch the atmosphere of the earth. So, for example, if one wears a five-and-a-quarter-carat ruby of a superior quality and precise cut, the rays of its associated planet—the sun—will touch the rays emitted by a ruby at an angle of ninety degrees.

However, to validate my hypothesis, I experimented on these gems. Daddy was the obvious first choice. He struggled hard to get a promotion in his job. Every year, even though he was eligible and deserving, this promotion never came to be. He often complained about his nearing retirement. I scrutinised his astrological diagrams and figured that the sun's position was weak in his chart and therefore triggered obstructions in the house for career and work. I asked my father to wear a ruby. Within three weeks, the letters of recommendation needed for a promotion arrived. His endorsement came through in six months. The ruby served as a filler, patching up a gaping hole.

Next, I experimented on my paternal aunt and uncle. Their health remained stable for many years, too. Gemstone therapy became a part of my consultations and remedies. A case to note is that of Raju Bhai Zaveri, a gem specialist in Mumbai. Twenty-five years ago, doctors warned him of a weak heart, later discussing a bypass surgery. I looked at his birth chart and recommended that he wear a red coral of an equilateral triangle shape that was 52.25 carats in weight. Nineteen years on, he is still alive and kicking, with no need for surgery. I think he does not let go of it now because of the placebo effect.

Since then, I take time to study, observe, and understand as much as possible, before I offer a healing yagya, a precious gem, or a few encouraging words. I walk the distance to another's world for a better chance at communication. I accept limitations and encourage my closest friends and family to face their experiences because we learn the most from difficult situations. Maturity filters in. But for those who despair, I warn them gently ahead of a roadblock or situation, bracing them mentally to meet the future.

A young man came for an intuitive astrology consultation in 2015. After a few personal questions, he asked about his parents' health. I predicted his father's death in five years. I also suggested his father wear a coral to lessen the impact of suffering and pain before his death. That was it.

Recently, the man's father ended up in hospital with severe symptoms of Covid-19 at the age of fifty-nine. The son called me for help, but there was nothing I could do there except a few kind words. I informed them of a critical transit period until the 19th of the month. If he survived that, there might be hope. I performed a fire ceremony to relieve him of the pain. The man died a few days before the 19th of the month.

The confused young man struggled with his mind. 'Do you think if my father wore the coral, he may have been less susceptible to the virus?' he asked. Well, this was one way to look at it. He was feeding his guilt and blaming a poor memory. But birth and death are not in our hands. We cannot compromise these two gateways. There is so much I forget personally and then remember later when things happen. Acceptance of our limitations helps growth and a better awareness in the future.

After that day in college, I learnt a valuable lesson; to look more closely at life. I open my eyes wider to know why situations occur in an environment the way they do. I dig into the underlying causes, pick up the vibrations in peoples' voices, apply astrology and intuition, and approach a situation more holistically. As much as possible, I integrate wholly while I think, talk, perform, and live my day.

We can interpret you,
for centuries to come
much like bowing in reverence.
We can feel your presence near and far,
yet no one may own you.
We can see the colours
of your fragrance high and low,
yet no one may touch you.
Your being nurtures creation
steady
infinite
eternal
flawless
whole
enduring
rejoicing.
When I start writing of you
I can keep writing of you

it just never ends,
eternal
eternal
eternal.

12

A Turtle Retreats

In quiet spaces, sound travels deeper into the subconscious. Exposed to the faintest echoes, a tranquil brain receives and identifies sound waves more intelligibly. When in maun, I experience deep sounds emanating from an undefined centre and while chanting, I feel the echo of each syllable reverberate in my bones. Tingling vibrations rush through my nerves and veins. Effortless and joyful, I never want to let go.

The knowledge of sound is one key to a vast abundance of intelligence and insight. In the state of *naad* or cosmic vibration, sound constantly moves in waves with high and low pulsations; something we often observe in a clear echo. While chanting internally, I bathe in echoes of a different kind; not the usual reverberation but specific phonemes that initiate a subtler expression of frequency. I feel nourished to the core, and this reflects in the external body, creating a visible attraction. It also enables me to visualise colour more vividly. I feel the brightness of the sun on my forehead with my eyes closed or when it is dark outside. This is because light and colour travel through space at much higher frequencies than heavier objects, such as stone.

Just as nature thrives in the amalgamation of sounds—the patter of rain, the rumble of thunder, the rustle of winds, the cry of a peacock, or the neighing of a horse—similarly, specific sounds influence different layers of the body and mind. Esoterically, in the *Devimahatmaya* traditions, thirty-seven seed sounds exist in the known universe. When chanted with precise intonation, these sounds induce a variety of sensations within the energy vortexes in an elemental body. The interplay of the tongue on meridian points, our lips in motion, the nasal passage, the throat, and the breath, all link to the brain stimulating hormonal secretions in the glands. A high frequency generated through repetitive chanting activates the cells in a body much like pulsating drumbeats. This produces feverish sensations, and each cell in the body feels sensitised.

However, these stages demand a level of discipline, focus, intent, and practice. So where does one begin? Perhaps at the most personal level—the breath. Without this precious commodity, you and I cannot communicate. The process, aspect, state, and degree of the inhalation, pause, and exhalation are what I call the dynamics of breathing; an indispensable, non-negotiable system which remains in motion constantly. There are three dominant *avasthas* or stages: *purak* or inhalation, *kumbhak* or retention, and *rechak* or exhalation.

The great yogis of the past acknowledged this cyclic intervention as a miracle of the breath. But busy humans, lost in thought and action, do not stop to wonder. We mostly breathe unconsciously throughout one cycle of twenty-four hours unless a virus interferes. In contrast, while breathing with awareness, we draw forth lighter sensations or aura available in the atmosphere. This is the law of attraction.

When singing or chanting, one focuses on the breath, transforming the act into a conscious process. When I make a prediction, chant, perform a yagya, or conduct a meditation, I enter a meditative state in the subconscious, aligning with the dynamic motion of breathing. This creates an aura, a brilliance, or a halo that emanates from the mind and expands through the body and its surroundings. The aura of those who have developed their minds is extremely effulgent. It can travel long distances and affect many persons who come under its influence.

So, what do we mean by a developed mind? A mind that is mostly in a state of awareness . . . awareness of the breath. Personally, mantra chanting has been a valuable tool for aligning the mind with the breath. The chanting of mantras—a cluster of sound formulas—corresponds to certain frequencies in nature. For instance, when uttering chants in a concentrated stance, the related sound frequency generates from a centre point in the atmosphere, spreading outward in an expanding circle. As it moves, this vibration creates an expansive funnel of light which encircles the utterer from head to toe. It builds a protective shield. The practitioner can then chant mantras and access forces that propel the elements—wind, water, earth, fire, and the atmosphere. Once the external aligns with the internal, an ever-present dormant force strengthens its hold within the body of a seeker. After decades of rigorous practice, I have gained access to hidden keys. The forces of nature come alive within me and reverberate through my being.

Let us take this concept a step further by dissecting the commonly known sound 'aum' into three unique notes:

A: Aakaar—shape or form.

U: Ukaar—the primordial inhale of a creative energy or life force.

M: Makaar—the primordial exhale, relative to decay, and renewal at the tail end of aum.

Thus, Aum is an invitation for an alignment, the coming into form or into shape. ॐ, written in the Devanagari script with a distinct dot, a crescent, two half circles, and a trail, represents a whole. The script formation also denotes the five elements, the five senses and the five forms of energy in a being. When visualised as ॐ, it opens a channel or a tunnel one may travel through from the known to the unknown. A powerful seed sound, absolute, self-sufficient, and independent, *Aum* is enough to refresh or balance one's personal existence within the macrocosm. It holds a profound possibility because the elaborated sound of '*Aum*' represents the underlying thought-form of a universal life-force.

It is the innate nature of light to expand. Energy illuminates the internal self and the external surroundings just as a single spark from a matchstick lights up a dark tunnel. When your practice deepens, the heart and mind find peace, and an effulgence appears on the exterior. Gradually, one expands in this state, becoming more in tune with what naturally surrounds us, ultimately merging with the eternal light—that which you and I are a spark of.

When I chant Sanskrit mantras repeatedly, I cross a bridge, walking into a deep unstruck silence, where all external commotion fades away. From *aahat*—peripheral sounds to *anahat*—a quiet expansive centre. I dissolve to align with *naad yog*, a continuous wave between the microcosm and the macrocosm. I feel like the silken thread that strings together the 108 seeds of a mala.

I began experimenting with the *Vistaarit* mantra—the expansion of a mantra—in April 1978. The first time I repeated the Ganpati mantra a hundred thousand times, it took two-and-a-half years. I noted it takes 926 rounds of repeating one mantra with a 108-beaded mala to get the numbers right. As a teenager, I had little to worry about and easily lost my sense of time and space while chanting. I completed a repetition—*jaap*—while staying silent each week from the sunrise on a Wednesday to thirty five hours later on a Friday morning. Soon enough, I willingly awaited those hours when I could live and breathe within myself like a baby in a womb.

Like any study, the knowledge of a mantra requires a methodical approach. The correct pulsation of the uttered sound, the intonation, the corresponding colour in relation to the focus point (a particular centre in the body), rhythm, repetition, consistency, and intent are essential to the practice. While reciting mantras, imagine a triangle shape with a focal point in the centre of this figure. This is you or the individual. The triangle serves as an anchor, traditionally termed as the *yantra*. The sounds uttered are the *mantra*. The individual, the sounds, and her/his focus expand in unison to the periphery of an equilateral triangle in a million rays. A transformation occurs, an intangible expression manifests. A throbbing occurs from within to the edge and back. The individual state alters, it expands, and one discovers a result. This result is broadly termed tantra.

A few years later, in 1986, I dived deeper into two ancient scripts: *Yajur Veda,* a treatise on mantras, and a transcription of *Soundarya Lahiri*, another Sanskrit text which literally translates as 'a wave of beauty'. The latter holds a descriptive analysis of formulas; one hundred coded Sanskrit verses or mantras with one common aim—the realisation of a result. This was an extremely desirable position for me. I wanted to find a way to assist people with difficult predicaments or find solutions directly rather than leaving them with just predictions.

Through an intensive process, I mastered the sounds of mantras to the extent that the risen vibrations are alive within me. These frequencies, constantly kindle within me just like a campfire on a dark night. This bonfire is slightly different though; it does not die out but remains lit within me all the time with a daily dose of care. Each time I use a formula of mantra for a specific solution, it depletes slightly within me. Then, like refilling a half-filled cookie jar, one must methodically chant a tenth part (to a million) of the activated mantra, thus ensuring its preservation in the body. In the last three and a half decades, I have devised sixty-four different formulas of mantras for various healing purposes.

You may wonder what 'alive within' suggests. Just as specialised study and decades of experience facilitates expertise in the respective field, similarly, intense research and practice of the occult studies expand common vision into an elaborated view. When this happens, all aspects of nature come alive; the elements are alive, colours are alive, knowledge is alive, and so is sound. Such dimensions are elusive yet accessible to any being who cares to move from the edges to a deeper centre.

As human beings, many wish to manifest this revelation into their personal self. I believe it is important to spend time with the basics first. The mantras for the Sun, in their first capacity, influence the physical steadiness of the body. We can then refine the sounds further for other physical aspects of nourishment and such. The mantras for the oceans (water) affect sexual compatibility and the attraction of life towards one another. Mantras for the moon correspond to the mind and the mental stability of a human. Mantras for the earth touch all of matter and the material world. Finally, the mantras for fire establish purification, harmony, and creative expansion among all beings. I compare this to the elementary study of any kind, the foundations that are important pillars to build upon. Learning and the expansion of the self is a process of lifetimes and there is nothing but time.

Personally, I went through a phase when being intuitive, reading astrological charts, and predicting was just not enough.

Sometimes, my predictions caused more grief because I saw the impending trouble. Obviously, I wanted to find purpose in it all. For instance, how could I aid a person in a positive way if the birth chart suggested a severe accident which could break the spinal cord into three pieces?

Astrology and intuition simply inform. That's all it does. What more could I do to assist with precautions or any level of preparedness? This is where the occult and its results, which is tantra, came into my life. I combine sounds (mantra chanting) with the invocation of an element (yagya or fire ceremony) to soften the blow a person might endure mentally and physically through a crisis. On 4 October 2007, Renu Gupta, a close friend in Jaipur, called frantically to inform me of her son who was critically ill in hospital. He had stopped responding to medication. For two months, I performed healing ceremonies applying a specific combination of mantras. Then one morning in the first week of December, the boy just got off the bed and ran out of his room. I met the boy soon after in his home. He said, 'In the hospital, I often found myself wandering in a maze of tunnels unable to find my way out, till I met an aged silver-bearded man dressed in white, who held my hand and guided me through.'

It is important to mention that no practitioner of the occult may alter determined events through these techniques. This is not possible, not at all. Change lies in the hands of a predetermined phenomenon. Through accessing subtle frequencies, in this case, mantras, fire ceremonies, astrology, and intuition, it becomes possible to minimise the detrimental effects of certain events or the severity of suffering in the larger well-being of humanity. Such alternate techniques that may connect a conscious thought with nature's intelligence have survived centuries of denial and superstition. A deeply conditioned patriarchal society continues to ignore the opportunity of diving into a subtler world of possibilities and probabilities. Women folk all over the world have been subjected to torture for venturing into areas that invoke a creative power. They become a threat to the physical superiority of a man.

I want to highlight the common perception of the occult as mythical, veiled, and fearful. In the mid-1990s, Hanegraaff devised a new definition for occultism: 'A category in the study of religions, which comprises all attempts by esotericists to come to terms with a disenchanted world or, alternatively, by people in general to make sense of esotericism from the perspective of a disenchanted secular world.'

In my experience, the study of the occult lays emphasis on alchemy. Behind all material phenomena, there is an interplay of powerful forces in the background that emanate from a centre. An in-depth study of this hidden dynamism or occult enables a magnetic pull towards this centre. But what is this 'centre'? This illusionary centre is the deepest core of the known universe or the womb from where life force springs forth.

A radio journalist once questioned if such techniques interfere with the natural cycle of an individual's journey. Well, I find evidence in the profound ways of nature. If there is poison or disease, then an antidote, a solution, or a remedy often exists at arm's length. For example, if a person incurs a sting with poison ivy, we mostly find a cure in the Jewelweed flower which grows nearby. The proximity of these bioactive trees is unique. The Bassa people from Cameroon use a flowering tree called strophanthus gratus to poison the tips of their arrows. The antidote, Alstonia boonei, carried in pouches to safeguard against the poison, comes from a tree found close to the first. Similarly, if you have stomach pain, both medicine and doctors are readily available. When we meet with an accident, police and doctors arrive and assist in most cases. So, would you call these interferences in your journey or help? Also, often there is no help. Why? Is it a missed opportunity? I wonder because when help does not arrive, it often results in upheaval, revolution, destruction, and renewal. Perhaps this is a necessity too.

Another question I get asked is about the misuse of such ambiguous techniques for personal gain. Sadly, this is true. A practitioner's foremost study involves observing negative aspects within oneself. The continuous awareness of one's hidden personalities allows for a better understanding of the human predicament. Self-awareness leads to loving yourself and the other. But it takes immense effort to discipline one's mind. It is a constant which one cannot let go of till the last breath. I also advocate a need to legitimise such practices with mandatory accredited certification not based on caste hierarchy, socio-religious structure, or patriarchal practices, but with sound information, education, and responsibility.

A decade ago, I started paying more attention to the fire ceremonies I conducted. Normally, I encouraged people to connect with their desire, attraction, and resolution. I asked them to visualise corresponding colours to attract the energies available to us all. But gradually I began observing people closely during these sessions. Some relate to their intent instantly. Some are anxious and take time to relax. Others are distracted or just inquisitive about me and the work I do. I have also heard people complaining about the heat generated during fire ceremonies. The elderly and the more vulnerable occasionally feel agitated and uneasy.

Focus on a purpose requires effort. I knew this, but how does one facilitate others? Naturally, I began integrating all that I had learnt and practiced; the breath, the relevance of time, stars, mantra chanting, planetary positions, dominant colours, and the shifting cycles of the moon. Healing turned more meditative and had a similar effect to a fire ceremony. So, I initiated my first collective meditation session, inviting a few people. I started with the chanting of aum, gradually involving other aspects like external and internal time, rhythm, and pace. Personally, I enter familiar territory where silence descends even though the chants turn louder. After the first session, I observed how the channelling of sound influences meditation. This is because sound has an efficient effect, irrespective of the surrounding chaos. It resounds through the body and the environment just like a soulful melody.

Secondly, the human body constantly radiates and receives energy from its surroundings, its interactions, and its influences. In a collective of any kind, one less charged body benefits through an expanding energy generated in an area or a room of fifty people. Potentially, one or many persons may feel supercharged after such a meeting.

After a couple of meditation sessions, all conducted on the night of a full moon, I collected feedback. An overworked man felt eased, a chronic insomniac said she slept better, university students returned for another session with less anxiety than the first time, a woman with clinical schizophrenia was far more attentive, and a grandmother felt a renewed sense of devotion to life itself. And I felt excited.

Yet, I needed more evidence because I think meditation as an exercise or a weekly class is one more distraction for the busy, programmed mind of today. For example, although sitting with closed eyes in a meditation class, a mother still worries about her hungry child. She cannot silence the natural process of her thoughts. Similarly, how can a father meditate with a constant eye on the clock so that he can collect his child after school? Their common meditation is in the child's care. A natural thought forced to regress causes war between the emotional body and the intellect. Division is a hurdle that stops the flow, the unity and your uninterrupted connection to the self. Therefore, understanding one's own patterns and structure is the first step. Accept rather than constantly fight. Work with rather than against.

Spontaneity may then become your key to living in meditation. For instance, a young woman looks up, feels the tingle of raindrops on her face, and breaks out into a wild jig. A little girl on a bicycle sings her heart out as her long tresses sway in the breeze. A professor enthrals a captivated audience on the mysteries of the universe. A carpenter carves a log of wood into a beautiful sculpture and a young man laughs like thunder, oblivious to the surrounding quiet. They are all involved, motivated, attentive, present, and aware. Similarly, when writing, one enters a world unique to the writer. All else fades or disappears.

Vivekananda contemplated every spoken sentence. That was his meditation. His teacher, Ramakrishna, meditated on every aspect of creation as the mother. Freedom was Nelson Mandela's constant focus. Service was Mother Teresa's meditation. Singing devotional songs was my Maa's contemplation. She often lost her sense of time or space. This was her meditation.

So, what is meditation? When I sit in the garden at dawn, looking at a rose bush, I lose myself in the petals, the vine, the thorns, and the shape of a budding flower. At night, I look at the stars and I count them. I am not thinking or trying to assess their names or origins. The millions of stars I see, have no names to call each other with. A rose does not know it has a name; humans call it a rose. When the sun appears, I bow down to its beauty. But the sun does not know it is beautiful. It just is. The sun, the stars, and the rose are all present. This presence is what I call meditation.

I started a meditation workshop with young students at Manipal University, Jaipur. One of them posed a question about the efficacy of meditative practices. I asked her to place self-examination at the forefront of all activity, to introspect her own actions for the next week, and to detect what she thinks, what forms her decisions, opinions, and beliefs. Question all your thoughts—I said to her. I also suggested she write her observations in a diary.

I believe meditation begins in a deeply personal space, and as a result, one encounters what they seek. The universe echoes the individual desire. If you sing, your universe sings. If you dance, you find dancers. When you open up to love, you meet love. In anger, the world resonates with anger. When quiet, the world becomes quiet with you. And when you are vulnerable enough, you drop into yourself. You meditate.

Slowly, gently, with feelings so soft,
I have etched you once again.
Time took a few turns, and years later
love bounced back in my blue eyes.
Slowly, gently, for you,
I caressed all your triumphs.
Footstep after footstep
when I feel hopeless
you hold me steady.
What an incredible knack you have
to make me smile, so I can
breathe like a vine, fragrant all over.
You are so alive within me
as if you are the idea, and

you are the attitude.
How will I express my gratitude to you
word for word?
Yet clearly, you are,
So . . . I am.
For you are
the axis of my life.

13

The Quintessence of Generosity

I am the oldest in our large family of six children—five sisters and a brother. When we sit together along with our families, it is an absolute riot. We share stories, news, and casual rounds of gossip. The atmosphere lightens me up like nothing else. Sister-friendships are often like a pack of assorted candies—sugary, bitter-sweet, delightfully tangy, brightly coloured bites of goodness and comfort. Each relationship has its seasons but never as unique, alive, and electric as that of sisters. Seetu, my youngest sibling, is more like a pampered daughter, while Madhu and Geeta are like the exquisite blue moon nights I always look forward to.

My sister, Vanita, is three years younger and we went to Prem Shanti School together, often walking through the centre of a park. One afternoon, Vanita stopped to look into a tall metal basket hanging between two poles. The basket was littered with dry leaves.

'Is it a swing, Baby?' Vanita asked.

'Look, Vanita,' I said, pushing the basket like a swing, 'it is.'

'Do you think I could sit in it for a ride? Please, that will be fun,' she asked.

I held her wrist and put on a serious face. 'You come back another day Vanita and when no one is looking, try swinging in it,' I said, walking her forward.

Vanita mostly believed what I said. We have such a laugh when she confesses it took her a long time to figure out that it was a waste bin and not a swing.

'I'm far more alert with Nirmala than I used to be, knowing she always has a trick up her sleeve,' she says now.

I was the inquisitive one who put her hand into everything without fear and naturally chose knowledge as my door to spirituality while Vanita constantly chooses a generous acceptance, and her spontaneous approach attracts the profundity of a spiritual life. Simple, steady, and giving, she holds her heart in the palms of her hands and invites everyone to drink from her overflowing cup. Her laugh, lighter than a feather, floats through the air, free for all to catch. Innocent and sometimes naïve, she grew to nourish all who touched her life.

***

It was a half-mile trek to and from school. On our way back in the afternoon, we often took a quick detour through *Amrudo ka Bagh* (the garden of guava trees). My friends climbed the small, clustered trees within this gated orchard, dodging the keepers, for want of a juicy guava. I never climbed a tree because I hated getting my hands or clothes dirty, but I coaxed others into it, often challenging them with a dare. I also convinced them I was standing guard and would make sure no one harmed them. The girls threw the juiciest guavas down to me while I practised the art of catching the fruit before it fell to the ground and if I missed, I blamed it on a poor throw. Filling up my school bag, I ran further out and waited for Vanita and my friends. Vanita often reminds me how I kept the choicest of guavas for myself and then shared the rest. She observed that but said nothing. When the gardener caught one of the girls stealing fruit, I went back and fought with him.

With my hands on either side of my waist, I said, 'You are the meanest, harshest man alive. How do you sleep at night knowing you are horrible to little hungry children?'

'But Bai Sa . . . you girls do this every day. I have a job here which I will lose if there are no guavas on the trees.'

'Stop the excuses. Our ten guavas will do nothing. Be nice to little children.'

'Go now and do not come again, please,' the poor man said with folded hands, while looking to the skies for forgiveness.

In a couple of days, I dared someone else to go. Vanita still remembers those carefree days when all the Sewani sisters sit together for a meal. When she comments how I dominated most choices in the family, my niece Ruchira flings her arms over me and says, 'No! Baby maasi organises and manages the entire family, and that is not dominating.' At that point, Shankar and the girls raise their eyebrows and pretend ignorance.

Yes, I inadvertently slid into the decision-maker's role and dictated most choices from the colours of our dresses, the paint on the walls, business decisions and my sisters' marriages. A role that should have been my mother's, but she was a quiet woman, kind, generous yet yielding and reverently subservient. Mother took care of everything in the background while father discussed all important matters with me, and I sure had an opinion about everything. Daddy acquainted me with every situation because he expected me to learn, understand and sacrifice. I was fourteen then and needed extra help with science at school, but my father gave the money to his siblings. For him, this was more important than science tuition. So, in the physics class, I sat quietly at the back of the classroom feeling nervous and insecure.

For a whole fortnight, the teacher called my name, asking questions on different topics. I could not answer because I did not understand. Physics was like an intricate puzzle impossible to unravel. My frustration poured out of me when a month later, I just stood there with tears washing my flushed cheeks. After the class, Upma, a girl who never spoke to me, asked why I was crying so much. Gradually, I opened up to her, asking questions and taking help with science. Upma was soft-spoken and confident. We interacted for a year and a half whenever I needed help or when she saw me struggling. Her open heart and generosity drew me to her.

Decades later, in 2016, I answered a call and heard the same generous voice on the other end. 'Hello, Upma. How did you find my number?' I asked.

'How do you know it is me, Nirmala?' Dr Upma said.

'That does not matter, Upma. I just know. Let us meet soon,' I said.

She came to my office in Jaipur for a cup of tea the next afternoon.

'Nirmala, I was so surprised to read your name in the papers. I first saw your picture in 2010 in a newspaper I was reading in between patients. I wondered. Is this the same Nirmala? She looks familiar. But how can it be? Nirmala was shy and quiet in class. Deep in such thoughts, a patient entered, and I put the paper in a drawer. Then I saw your picture again a month ago, and this time, I just had to track you down. You have travelled far, and I cannot believe that the girl with a flushed face and quiet tears has grown so much through sharing with others,' she said.

'I still remember those days when you helped me through equations and problems in physics,' I said with a smile.

'Well, I felt a powerful urge to help you because I sensed something awkward in your silence. I felt the inner conflict but had no awareness to understand it better,' she said.

Dr Upma and I meet when we can and share a rare friendship that has its own unique fragrance from our past. When I meet her, the air changes. It transports us both back to the age of fourteen yet nurtures my present. I talk to her without inhibitions, and we share without boundaries.

'When I meet you, Nirmala, I feel waves travelling up my bloodstream. This is essentially a secretion of hormones, endorphins, and dopamine, that work as a neurotransmitter. A feeling of pleasure envelops me, and I realise momentarily that the smallest part of life is the same in essence.'

'You are right, Dr Upma. In my world, it is.'

I admire her generous sensitivity too, which did not cave into the rigours of a prejudiced society and its beliefs. It helps me continue my search for new connections, while sharing from one person to the next.

I also travel once every year to Jammu, a city in the Himalayan mountains. I visit people who have stood with me through my struggles, decisions, joys, and sorrows. Each Diwali I perform a healing yagya for the family, ringing in a new year. This is one place where I leave all responsibilities behind and get some respite from my schedules, meetings, and positions. I am pampered to the hilt, but more than that, I love sharing notes with Lata. A quiet woman who understands the preciousness of time far better than most.

'The way my life has turned out, Nirmala, I am grateful for all the miracles,' she said recently.

'Miracles are a limitation of the mind, a myth. They do not exist. The time difference between an action undertaken and its result varies. Years of study result in a postgraduate doctoral degree. I perform a healing yagya because of thirty-five years of constant effort; no miracle there. And you, dear Lata, have spent decades nurturing the environment you feel grateful for today,' I playfully nudged her one late afternoon as we had tea in her garden.

Lata may be the axis of her family, yet she holds an invisible presence. After years of a liberal selfless attitude, she now emanates a love one cannot resist. Yet, Lata bypasses the effort. As humans, we often forget the relationship between time and consequence. A simple comparison could be the baking of a cake. Mix all the ingredients in the right proportions, bake to the right temperature, and in an hour the result shows in your delighted face. When results are immediate, we mostly know the reasons. However, when outcomes take twenty years, the action performed fades with time and memory. The mind shifts and changes through these long years. Initially, we brand events as a miracle because we simply do not remember the causes. Then the brain interprets results either rationally or euphorically, often proclaiming a miracle. Thirdly, the principle of cause and effect persists, akin to the earth's organized path. There is a constant intent, a focus, and a purpose in the macrocosm with a consequence way larger than human perception. It is an accumulation or a result in time.

I remember when I first visited the ashram, Dr Mishra was sixty-two, and I was thirteen. A middle-aged caretaker, Sukanya, and I were the two women in that environment. I never understood her relationship with Dr Mishra.

One afternoon, I commented, 'Sukanya is so ugly and short, and you are so tall and beautiful. She is weird and no match for you.'

Dr Mishra was gentle in his response. 'Nirmala, you will understand as you grow older. She will deliver a purpose when the time comes. She is a mother who serves selflessly.'

This was true. In my heart, Sukanya, the generous caretaker of the ashram holds a position at least three places higher than Dr Mishra. Her care and respect for the day and people are difficult to emulate. Like many teenage girls, I spent enough time choosing dresses, accessories, and shoes for the day. I braided my long hair with matching baubles and ribbons and did not step out until I liked what I saw in the mirror. Quick and efficient, I did not spend hours dressing, but I just knew how I wanted to present myself. In contrast, Sukanya walked with her shoulders bent, her hair messy, dull, and always oiled flat, her clothes clean but careless, and she wore the same slippers day in and day out. Her attire was awkward. In my eyes, she was this dishevelled figure pottering about the place with little care or concern for her own presence. In fact, I thought she moved around much like an annoying shadow that followed all of us wherever we stood or sat in the ashram.

But the same Sukanya cooked, cleaned, and took charge of all big and small jobs in that place. She was everywhere. Her kindness was so palpable that I would shy away from her. Though thin and frail, she was as steady as a tall mountain. The boys loved her, joked with her, teased her, and ignored her orders, but mostly appreciated her attitude.

We often heard her commanding tone a mile away and imitated her. At other times, we heard nothing; a silence descended on the ashram as she massaged Dr Mishra's feet. When he slept, she stood guard outside his room, making sure no one made a sound. She gestured to us, making funny postures while we mimicked and bothered her. Much later, I learnt she was in love with Dr Mishra. She found her sunrises in his needs, desires, and wishes till he left her alone with the long sunsets of Rajasthan's desert.

In retrospect, Sukanya is the most beautiful interaction by which I have learnt. Through her, I understood the beauty of a woman. She searches for her identity in the generous seeking of love. I felt the rhythm of feminine emotions better; feelings that steer the softest impulses of the anahat—the central cavity. I observed Sukanya's quiet presence, her strength, her resilience, and a much finer quality—her generosity. Years later, when

I visited the ashram, I observed a fragility in her endurance. She gave her all till she too merged into the sunset, fulfilling her purpose. Through Sukanya, my mother, and each woman I held hands with, shared with, and grew with, I have learnt the infinite capacity of a mother. The inherent nature of a mother is intuitive, simple, and complete. She is whole. It is from her wholeness that she nurtures a baby in the womb. Madhu, two years younger than Vanita, consistently sang verses and words of wisdom to her unborn. Her boy, Akshay, birthed gently into this world and carries with him a steady calm and devotion wherever he goes. A whole new being birthed from the generous womb of a woman.

A man gives too and is generous too. Yet he gives only until the day he walks away searching for his own identity. Sukanya seeks too, but only love. Endlessly willing in her duties, her day revolved around the man she loved. And when he walked away to attain his goal, she stayed behind to take care like a generous custodian. Sukanya was a little matchstick that lit every candle on the way, burning herself in it quietly. Simply. Silently.

I have now understood Yogesh Mishra's words better: 'She is a selfless mother.'

Your smile and your giggles
so innocent to this day
yet when tides turn, you teach us how to be.
Barkha, Deepa, Saroj, or *Sugandha*
is there worth in a name?
The strength of a woman is alive in you
it keeps you aflame.
Now

you lead the way,
for us,
all of us.
You triumph,
never closing the window of hope.
Bursting with dreams,
you dream a dream.

14

Standing in the Doorway

'Do you think I might get a promotion at work soon, Nirmala?' My father asked.

'I don't think so Daddy, not for a while at least,' I said.

That was it. I spoke too quickly. It was unacceptable and my words upset him.

'You must pay more attention to what you say, Nirmala,' he said, leaving the room in a huff. It took a full day to calm him down. While reading an astrological chart and predicting, I do not bounce between objectivity and favour. People-pleasing is not one of my traits while clearly, my father did not move from his position as a parent. Therefore, the clash and frustration.

It did not matter whether my words and predictions were right or wrong but a reprimand in some form often awaited me. It took several years for me to understand a father's struggle between instilling a strong foundation in us while also protecting his girls from societal expectations. He was a determined parent to five daughters born into a tradition where a baby girl breathes in the limitations of caste, gender, bias, and subservience in the womb of her mother.

My father challenged his environment while teaching us to grow as independent thinkers. Also, he knew I was digging my heels into a deep-rooted patriarchal profession that is inherently biased to a woman's perspective. The study of the ancient scriptures, Vedic astrology, mantras, philosophy, and yagyas are precious heirlooms of Brahmin Hindu men. Cancelling women's participation at the outset ensures their monopoly in a lucrative business. Thus, my father's dilemma surfaced more than often.

Yet, he also admired my efforts, always supporting and encouraging me. Like many of his time, he too was a son of the partition, forced out of a wealthy household at nine. In Pakistan, our family followed ancestral traditions. It was an honour to announce the firstborn as a devout Sikh; a Sardar presented for the duties of the gurudwara. But my grandfather could not accomplish that because partition closed many doors. Probably, a sense of devotion or debt lay buried in the subconscious, so when Daddy looked at me, his first child, this trampled loyalty showed its face again. Within that frame, it became irrelevant to him that I was a girl child.

Daddy's picture of a brave, fearless warrior Sardar helped me. He offered me the freedom to develop as an individual. He respected my ideas, opinions, and authority on relevant topics. From an early age, I sat with his friends and colleagues discussing literature, religion, philosophy, and politics. I was a part of most decision-making at home, within the larger family and for the wider community as well.

My father had a small library of books in his study. He reminded us often, 'If one does not dive into literature, he or she remains bereft of the required sensitivity in the intrinsic construction of one's personality.' I repeat his words to the next generation. I read Anton Chekhov's works on realism, the philosophical anarchism of Leo Tolstoy, the socialism of Maxim Gorky, and great thinkers from the Indian subcontinent like Nirala, Jai Shankar Prasad, Shivani, Ismat Chughtai, Manto, Padma Sachdev, Mrinal Pande, Rabindranath

Tagore, Amrita Pritam, and R. K. Narayan. I was lucky with the exposure because of my father's interest in literature. Later I studied and researched subjective material such as the Sanskrit treatises—*Vrihat Parashari* (astrological treatise), *Uttar Kalamrit,* (Vedic astrology), and so on. Occasionally, I heard the modern philosophy lectures of Acharya Rajneesh and read the metaphysical works of Arvind Yogi, an expert in para psychology.

It was a daily mid-evening ritual, eagerly anticipated by all of us. We followed my father—all four sisters, my brother Shankar, and myself—into his study, staying there until hunger drove us back to Maa for dinner. On one such afternoon, running my fingers through a row of hardback books, I chanced upon a tiny booklet crushed between heavyweights. Holding it between my palms, I patted its compressed form back into shape. Settling back on the rug, in the best space between my siblings, I read the title on the light grey dusty paperback: *Thoughts of Power* by Swami Vivekananda. It was a small book with just eleven short verses. I read it in less than five minutes, shut the pamphlet, and held it between my palms. Counting to ten, I opened it again, and the words flashed in my face: 'In studying books we are sometimes deluded into thinking that thereby we are being spiritually helped; but if we analyse the effect of the study of books on ourselves, we shall find that, at the utmost it is only our intellect that derives profit from such studies, and not the inner spirit.'

I sat with the words for a long time. The shuffling and whispering from my siblings faded away. I read the verses once more and felt every word implode in my nervous system. Every muscle in my body, every cell in my brain activated as if hooked into a charging socket much like a dead mobile phone that springs back to life when plugged in. I read the verses repeatedly.

Another verse from the same booklet remains personal and extremely alive in my research: 'Take up one idea, make that one idea, your life; think of it; dream of it; live on that idea. Let the brain, muscles, nerves, and every part of your body be full of that idea and just leave every other idea alone. This is the way to freedom, and this is the way great spiritual giants are produced.'

That afternoon, I discovered an intimate freedom in the words I read. To this day, I am still working on that one idea which might lead me to my expansion, freedom, liberation, and *moksha*. All these possibilities opened up because of my father. He was clearly my first teacher. He nurtured a seed with care, watered it with individuality, and afforded it with adequate free space. He held my tiny hand every day, inculcating a sense of respect for myself and my thoughts. I sensed no limitations on being female. I could contemplate creative ideas, assimilate my thoughts with clarity, and recognise my inner spirit while also interacting with the larger world.

Amma, my father's mother, often stood in the doorway, waiting for my father to pass through. With both hands on either side of her hips for effect, she said, 'Girls in our family are married off at seventeen, and your girl wears short skirts, stares into a stranger's eyes, and even touches the hands of older men all day.' My sisters and I giggled while imitating her, so she would raise her voice louder, yelling for all to hear, 'You will see for yourself. One day she will give the family a bad name.' My father always shook his head but said nothing. Another time she commented, 'Now who will marry the younger girls if the eldest has such ways, I wonder?' Vanita had an arranged marriage before me, and this was funny because it jolted Amma's poor heart out of place.

Before we moved to Jaipur, my father lived in Ajmer with Maa, Amma, and his siblings. A road trip to this city is one of my favourite drives. I often lose myself in the red, orange, and fuchsia bougainvillaea growing wildly along the drive. With their vines twisting intricately into one inseparable chain, these blossoms cascade down the ghastly pale Aravalli hills in a defiant feminine display.

I take a deep breath while walking through the dargah bazaar. Delicate strands of Rosa Bourbonia waft through the narrow lanes of the bazaar. A fragrance like none other. I walk from shop to shop buying herbs, oils, and incense for ritual ceremonies; handmade *agarbatti* sticks and rose incense cones wrapped in soft tissue, pure rose oil in small glass vials, and I also buy some *gulkand* (rose petal jam).

I visit Ajmer Sharif—a Sufi dargah—annually. The sight transports one into the literal embodiment of the word 'diversity' if you wish. It is a high-pitched frenzied chaos one cannot ignore. Standing slightly away on a red and green stripe *dhurrie* in the well-shaded veranda, I watch people carrying straw baskets on their heads, hundreds of them, big and small, filled with rose petals and other offerings, making their way through the disorder. The sweet-scented waves from the Rosa Bourbonia petals mesmerise me till I am nudged back by a girl child pushing her way through the visiting saints, shopkeepers, women, and old people, all jostling for space, a prayer, and a voice. It contradicts the movement of the eye; multitudes of cross-cultural faces in all hues and tones, walking through a large open complex at an irritatingly oblivious pace on the one hand to a nervous rush of necking their way through the narrow door into the inner sanctum of the shrine. Nothing makes sense yet the crowds glide forward as a collective, each one managing a glimpse of the tomb within. Feverish exaltations of the attendants and devotees move millions constantly through these chambers. Rarely is there a mishap. The fragile thread of faith weaves into a timeless thick rope each time another foot enters the cramped space. A sacred sanctity created by none other than a steady stream of life itself.

Native to this land, I am vulnerable yet strengthened in its commotion. I step out of the dargah to a vast canvas, stretching beyond the peripheral vision of my eye. Animals, colourful food stalls, babies being carried by wee toddlers, women prancing in their colours, disabled men and women on all sorts of coping mechanisms, competing shopkeepers shouting over beeping horns, neon-coloured dresses hanging like carousels, haggling guides, rickshaws, eager pilgrims, and so much more. I take another deep breath to renew my sense of adaptability in a defiantly flexible environment.

I also observe a profound acceptance, a quiet surrender, and a daring hope amid the chaos. Every aspect moves, influencing and operating the understated system. No problem, and no fear in the supposed masquerade of pandemonium. This is how I dare to describe the word 'real,' where spaces for pretence and politesse simply do not exist. Driving past the street in downtown Ajmer, where I spent the first four years of my life, I turn back to see reconstructed houses dotted with vague remnants of my childhood. Much has changed.

After my father passed away, Maa often spoke of her early years in the Sewani family. She did not conceive for six years after marriage.

'Please Devi Maa, bless my daughter-in-law, or I will die without seeing my grandchild,' Amma prayed twenty-four by seven for divine intervention.

One summer evening in May 1964, Amma sat in the veranda with her straw fan, enjoying a cool breeze while waiting on my father. Maa watched her from the kitchen. Suddenly, Amma waved her arms in the air frantically, as if trying to brush away a fly. Then she looked at the skies above and said something.

Maa asked, 'Amma, who are you talking to?'

Pointing upwards, Amma said, 'I saw a little girl come down from the clouds. She says, "I will come as your daughter soon." But I'm too old now. I said to this girl as I saw her fade away.'

My mother laughed but felt sad at the same time.

But Amma said to Maa, 'I am sure you will conceive soon, and I will have a granddaughter.'

Maa says she heard a tone of inevitability in Amma's voice that evening. Faith, belief, and hope attach certainty to premonitions and visions. My mother conceived soon after and delivered a premature baby on 23 February 1965. I was a tiny, weak baby, and as my worried parents prayed, Amma commented, 'There is no need to fear. She is Ganga. She will survive.'

That star
shining brightest in the universe
that is you
A star shining for me
way above in the sky
but its glow encircles me
here
constantly
and whenever I want to say
something to you
I turn my gaze
to the blue sky
and look at that star shining
in a rare light.
I am face to face with you.

15
The Story of a Star

At the very core, I have an empirical affair with instinct, foresight, and intuition. Each person will have their own knowing through a gut feeling, a flash, or an inkling. A personal relationship with yourself. Yet instinct permeates all of life. It emerges through an elaborate weaving. A weaving of all of us; humans, animals, plants, oceans, stars, the rain, and the wind.

Reversing back to the beginning, I may compare my intuition to the opening and closing of a switch. Quick and short, sometimes momentary—a sudden zoom, a glimmer, and a flicker. As a child, I did not know its origin and because I was oblivious to what triggered it, I had no control over the flow or the outburst of an intuitive thought or picture. At best, it was a revelation. A gush, a flash of lightning or a sudden happening. But I distinctly heard each vibration in the reverberation of an echo. I voiced such thoughts and ideas that originated from mental flashes, physical vibrations, and colourful images. A flicker materialised as an idea, an instant decision, or a prediction.

Words fall short when trying to express strong feelings. It's a personal receptivity, a reflex, or an innervation. Something elusive and overly sensitive to touch. Hence, regardless of all the words I use to explain it, I cannot nail the intensity of a feeling.

Yet, I sense a force so grounded I cannot deny it. And it returns. Symbols, colours, and light trickle in. In those moments, a great clarity takes over. Information percolates in my nerve endings. I think it, perform it, or speak it. I have no choice. When I was younger, I had no idea how to stop it. Thank goodness, I have matured a little.

Most healthy babies are highly intuitive. An innocence, an allowance, so carefree in its conception, it lets the mystery of existence rain down. Often this first quality dissipates through a constant merging with immediate surroundings. Varying degrees of exposure in the local environment, permit, tame, or block access to a child's insight or ideas. An intelligent faculty that fades away in the overwhelming social edifices of conformity. Archetypal parents, grandparents, and the household are foremost at fixating on our views and behaviours. Indifferent peers, predisposed perceptions, rigid mannerisms, and a thousand instilled fears account for the disintegration of a conscious, integrated thought.

Thankfully, I ticked none of those boxes because of an open-minded father. From a young girl of seven to my adolescence, I thought, expressed, created, and performed from feeling; feelings and thoughts that raced through me into the external and back within. Constantly moving between a vibration, a frequency, a buzz, a continued excitement, a high till I heard the crescendo of a finer thought. Gradually, I developed an awareness of what I felt. A knowing grounding me like roots, penetrating deep into my physical and subtle bodies; my brain, emotions, and intellect. This steadiness became my strength, armour, and confidence in nothing but myself.

I access every vibration in a voice, essentially a mirror to one's subconscious, to a thought, to the past, the present, the future, and to a personality. Initially, I failed miserably at controlling my tongue and constantly saw it run a mile ahead of me. I existed in a common world, yet my world was so different. At nineteen, I spoke with a raw intensity that could embarrass so-called cultured folk. I gave honest feedback, never sugar-coated a word, and even though I was not harsh, I often came across as blunt. Mostly because I did not lie. I cared little for social mechanisms like loyalties, investments, or expectations. I still do not feed them. It could be anyone, a friend, colleague, or His Royal Highness of Jaipur, Durbar Bhawani Singh. I met him in the year 1987, just before he ran for the elections as chief minister of Rajasthan. My father knew his private assistant well. An aged gentleman, his name was Raghunath Singh and I addressed him as Dada hukum.

One day, Dada hukum came to our home with a question from the Durbar. It was about the elections. I said that His Royal Highness should not fight the election and predicted he would lose severely if he did. But Dada hukum visited again to book an appointment for the Durbar, a week in advance. I remember him marking the meeting in his diary and mine, even though we had a telephone.

On the day of the meeting, Durbar Bhawani Singh parked his entourage on the adjacent main road and walked unescorted to the fourth house in the street. He paced from the left to the right of the centre table in the living room. I watched his movements, glad that there was enough room between him and the armchairs by the wall.

I answered him and if Durbar asked the same question twice, I repeated the same answer. He argued that a large group of people had assured him of support in the elections. 'I have a fair chance of winning the seat,' he said.

'If a bunch of people could change what the stars say, I would be chief minister too. I have told you what the stars say. Yes, we may lessen the impact of the defeat, but that's about it,' I said.

Even though I was young, Durbar openly admired what he observed in me and respected my authority on the occult. The Maharaja of Jaipur understood astrology. He was a keen astronomer too. We often started the discussion with physical predicaments until it dissolved into a more existential pondering. In between such sessions, he also taught me how to make a good cup of English tea, or what we call black tea. I laughed at the audacity of labelling homegrown tea as English and not an austere English recipe that took the joy out of relishing a rich and slow infusion of tea leaves, spices, and milk.

'Nirmala, it is wise to learn the ways of the world,' he often said.

Anyway, Durbar lost the election. It devastated him. I suggested he feed his desire for politics through the backdoor. He became an ambassador soon after, salvaging his pride. I also recommended he wear a coral for his health. So, he asked me to find one that suited the purpose. All that was fine, but to have a stone worth its quality, one has to buy it. My father's monthly salary was seven thousand rupees. It fed an extended family of parents, siblings, his wife, and children. I got the coral on a credit note and waited patiently for the money. Gradually I learned to be more forthright with financial and social skills.

As for astrology, it is about calculations wherein planetary movements function as informants. Nothing more. Such movements like a new moon or a full moon do not convey any results. In addition, I am a human prone to error. I know little in comparison to the vast ocean of knowing and knowledge. But intuition sprouts from a source contrary to scholarly investments, worldly skills, and expectations. Therefore, it is unnerving. As a young woman, I spoke with unapologetic confidence. Dr Sunny Bakshi, a noted homoeopath from the more cosmopolitan city of Delhi, met me through a common friend in 1989 for consultation. An unusually tall, well-built man with a bright red turban looked down to where I sat in the little office I worked from in the centre of Jaipur.

'Yes, that will be me, Nirmala. Sit down,' I said.

'But you're too young,' he said without hesitation. I nodded and in less than two minutes, pieced his predicament to a tee. He wondered how I knew so much about his life.

'It is written all over you, Sunny. I just picked up the necessary information,' I said laughing so heartily that he joined in too. But by the end of our first session, I figured that he did not believe anything I had said. He called again because what I said came true. Soon he had more confidence in my words and a friendship blossomed between us.

Every time we spoke, he pestered me to visit Delhi and stay with his family. 'I feel a rare hope when I speak to you, Nirmala. You have the courage to say what others do not,' he said.

'I just say what I pick up in a voice.'

'You have so much potential, Nirmala. You cannot remain the content frog in a little pond. There is an ocean out there for you to discover.'

'I have never stepped out of Jaipur on my own.'

'It is not so difficult, Nirmala,' he said.

I asked my father to book me a bus ticket to Delhi. There was a week to go. I prepared a suitcase with all the clothes I loved. In the evening, I telephoned Sunny and made sure he wrote all the details of my arrival. I must have repeated everything at least five times. This was way before the convenience of instant and constant communication. Daddy and I arrived early at the bus station, and I was the first one on the bus. I took the second-row window seat behind the driver. I hardly made eye contact with anyone and waved to my father while hanging onto my bags. It took a while to relax although I did not let go of my bags for the entire seven-hour journey.

I had never felt nervous like this while predicting, counselling, or encountering strong-headed people and predicaments. I always knew how to be and what to do. But stepping out of my world had a strange, almost alien effect. The atmosphere felt different. When I let the wind rustle my hair through the open window, I sensed a new excitement. The speed with which the villages and towns passed my eyes spoke to me of a distinct vibration. A fresh energy.

I chanted all the way to Delhi for seven hours, clinging on to familiarity. The bus stopped at ISBT, the regional bus terminus in Delhi. Passengers hurried out while I sat there looking out of the window till I saw a tall man with a navy turban. I waved to him. As he came closer, I asked him to walk round to the door of the bus. When I saw him there, I stepped off with all my stuff.

I stayed at Sunny's home with his family and set up a little office to meet people there. Word spread fast through his acquaintances, and I began interacting with a unique set of people. It was a foreign territory where I hopped between strange mannerisms, peculiar ideas, and weird attitudes. Quickly realising my unfamiliarity with it all, I adapted when meeting all kinds of people; urban women, bureaucrats, young professionals, and entrepreneurs.

One evening, Sunny invited a senior politician for dinner who wanted to ask about his political future. 'When will I become the president of the country?' he asked.

'Just because you wear a turban, and you are a warrior Sikh does not mean you might become the president. This will never happen,' I replied.

My tone and careless words rightfully offended the man. Sunny spent the rest of the evening flattering him while I slid away to my room.

'Yes, I admire your courage, but you must tone it down and refine your words.' Sunny said the next day.

Pretence reveals our double standards. I was now bumping into it every moment. I observed and adapted quickly to a more ego-centric audience. I am more careful with words today and slightly wiser, dare I say. I simply nod, hoping my silence speaks for itself. After all, one's truth is relative; without a right or wrong.

Maun or the practice of silence became my armour. I observed more keenly hence a renewed lucidity and neutrality emerged from my words. I studied the purpose behind 'information'. Good information acts as a tool for an effective beginning. A significant start into the unknown. If I know, I am anchored and can deal with a situation better, whereas the unknown creates fear. It makes a person anxious and insecure, preventing one from stepping outside the boundaries of the known. In comparison, the phrase, 'I know' is a godsend; it is a relief. But, if one has the courage to whisper 'I do not know,' a possibility emerges.

Centuries ago, the key purpose of studying the astral world was to understand the changing seasons in nature. With information about the skies, farmers regulated their crops and agricultural produce thrived. Traders, sailors, and nomads speculated the stars and skies just like a satellite navigation system. Hence, the roots of Indian astrology lie in the study of stars and their terrestrial positions. It examines the unity of three universal principles in an organised movement—the sun, moon, and earth. When I first saw my father's friend draw out a birth chart with the essential aid of an Indian almanac, I fell in love with both the diagram he made and the mystery behind a specific way to access time and movement.

Fascinated with the casting of the Indian almanac at age nine, I wanted to understand what looked like an intriguing sudoku puzzle and I wanted to solve it. Its elaborated format revealed the position of the sun, moon, and other planets on a fixed latitude/longitude in context to a twenty-four-hour cycle. There is a basic difference between the modern calendar and the Indian almanac that I found interesting. Within the Hellenistic concept, a new day begins from a second after midnight while in the Panchangam, a new day starts at sunrise. Secondly, the Gregorian calendar bases its arithmetic on the sun's movement, summing up the solar year of 365 days, 5 hours, 48 minutes, and 46 seconds. The Panchangam uses a solar year but divides it into twelve lunar months with calculations based on the revolution of the moon around the earth. This affects the moon's changing shape and movement through the zodiac. These differences fascinated me as a nine-year-old. It highlighted the diversity of thought. There were so many ways to look at the same sun and moon.

Jyotish or Indian Vedic astrology, translates to 'the evolution of light.' The most distinguishing feature though is its reliance on pran or life force, the energy emanating in the cosmos, and its harmony with every living aspect of creation. The air we breathe is a conventional reminder that all of existence is sustained through the undisturbed alignment of pran.

Jyotish eulogises the sun as the cosmic eye, the core of a moving and unmoving universe. It portrays the moon as the mind of this life force. It further elaborates on how the phases of the earth's moon affect the deepest tendencies of all creatures. Indian astrology accounts for the movement of the sun, moon, and earth in concurrence with the planets and two imaginary *bindus* (dots): *rahu* and *ketu*. Rahu marks the beginning, while ketu is its polar opposite, marking the other end of the zodiac—the apparent path of the sun.

Thus, while making a calculation, an astrologer applies the movement of the planets and their attraction to the corresponding date, year, and time at birth to make a calculation. These equations then propose a line of action where a planet's placement intersects a birth chart. Basic astrological charts are widely available on computers because there is a method in the summation. A prepared diagram provides information about the location of the earth, stars, and planets at a precise year, month, date, and time in the twenty-four-hour cycle.

At the age of fifteen, I read ancient Greek astronomers, though I struggled to find Hindi translations. Interestingly, Ptolemy likened astrology to medicine. He said, 'Race, country, and the upbringing of an individual, all affect the personality, and the analogous positioning of the sun, moon, and planets at the precise time of birth are considered in administering a dose for a healthy mind and thought.' He also found immense value in the 'second' in terms of time, concentrating on the constant influences of the celestial bodies in the sublunary sphere, all explained in his astrological treatise, *Tetrabiblos*.

Such information deeply influenced my research in astrology and its application. I experimented on humans and animals in relation to earth time. We lived in a semi-detached house with a narrow, half-grass, half-paved back garden. In my most messianic phase, between 1984-88, I reasoned it was easier to fit in a small animal within the space and my busy schedule. I got two pet cats, a male and a female. I evaluated their detached behaviours in contrast to those of other creatures. This involved painstaking deductions of their emotional conduct and patterns in concurrence with sextiles, oppositions, and trines formed by planets at contrasting times of a twenty-four-hour period: dawn, noon, evening, dusk, and night.

I felt no apathy in putting my hands into the cat's basket where she lay in menstrual blood sometimes. It shocked Amma, who often complained to her goddesses for sending her a sorcerer instead of an angel. But I was excited because now the cat was pregnant.

It was a chilly winter morning when the cat birthed. I was preparing for a test at college, so I missed the birth of the first two kittens. I rushed out with the almanac, a stopwatch, and a notebook, as she delivered the next three. Later that evening, I prepared and studied the charts. The kittens birthed when the moon was in transit or at a point of void. This occurs when planetary positions are adrift, unfocused, and disconnected. I repeated the procedure for the next three years with the same results and deducted that it is at this point of inaction in planetary positions that most cats birth, which is partly responsible for their unique, solitary behaviours in extreme contrast to that of humans and other animals.

For the next four years, I expanded my research to further understand the shifts in human emotions and personalities as a direct consequence of lunar positions. Often, I got to look at a hundred different birth charts in a week. I studied a variety of situations, their influences on the mind and their effect on the body. The moon's movement has a deep impact on shifting personalities, the mind, creativity, and attitudes which influence our predicaments. As it transits from one zodiac sign to the next in approximately two days and a quarter, the moon touches all of nature including high tides and low tides, fish, worms, eagles, and the sudden mood swings in a person, often dramatic, and at times, extreme.

Let's look at a case study which shows the comparison between an associate's chart 'A' and mine. The configuration is identical except for one aspect—the moon. 'A' was born when the moon was in Libra, an air sign, and ten hours later, it moved into Scorpio, a water sign when I was born.

Person 'A' birth details: 7:00 a.m., 22 February and mine: 5:05 am, 23 February in the Gregorian calendar. The Panchangam considers my birth date as the 22nd of February because the sun surfaced an hour later at 6:05 a.m. Interestingly, during those ten hours, the moon shifted from an air sign to a water sign. Next, the ascendant moon in chart 'A' is in the eleventh house which denotes a tangible peak such as material wealth. On the other hand, mine is in the twelfth house along with the position of ketu. This represents an intangible pinnacle—the realised self. This one variant aspect influenced us differently as 'A' turned materially successful with immense financial power while I grew and matured with my knowing and knowledge. Both wealthy yet at opposite extremes.

From the spring of 1989 to 1992, I collaborated with two PhD psychology students, Poonam and Vikas, for their experimental thesis on the connections between human psychology, schizophrenia, and lunar phases. In the one hundred case studies we discussed, I found that depending on the planetary positions, a full moon affects the mental state of a person often resulting in insomnia, depression, and extreme split personalities (schizophrenia). Common examples are skin problems that may arise during a waning moon. This is due to the fading effect of the moon's rays, or on a moonless night, the immediate layers under the skin may flare up more with boils and filariasis. In the tick-tock of each second spent on this cyclic lunar journey, the moon constantly affects all aspects of birth, growth, decay, and rebirth on planet earth. The interdependence is so elusive, so silent in its functioning, that a busy mind ignores it as non-existent.

A new moon follows a night of complete darkness, a moonless night. It prompts a human to face his or her darkness within. In the light of a new moon, and a new dawn, the same moon showers the mind with renewed determination. A reshuffled energy. A brand-new opportunity.

The sensuous flute of a full moon lures me to a silent dance within. Its rays leave nothing untouched; plants, minerals, animals, fish, colours, rocks, oceans, mountains, rivers, and the human intellect, inviting everyone to bask in the sustenance offered. An effortless, profound, continuous gift devoid of any division or exclusion. I sing to this phenomenon. *Aum chandrayah namah;* salutations to the moon.

As part of the study, we researched another aspect of astrology that has a deep effect on the emotional state: *Grehan yog,* which translates to the knowledge of shadows. Partial and total eclipses of the sun and the moon come under this study. For an eclipse to occur, the alignment between the moon, earth, and sun must be precise. A near alignment results in partial and penumbra eclipses whereas complete alignment causes total eclipses.

Astrologically, the moon on its own represents a stable state of mind, steady emotions, and a mental equilibrium represented by an off-white hue. But the state of our emotions shifts in concurrence with a shadow. Ideally, there are three visuals in a birth chart that cause shadows: combination A—ketu and the moon, B—rahu and the moon, and C—Saturn throwing a shadow on the moon. These combinations cause a dark area between the rays of light and a surface. A grehan (eclipse) triggers mental imbalances, depression, insomnia, and nervous breakdowns. All these entwined influences disrupt a spontaneous emotion, creating an unknown upheaval in thought with heavier more agitated feelings. The body may also show signs of sudden ailments, respiratory change, and fevers. The impact or the height of this disorder depends on the strength of the eclipse from partial to a total eclipse.

While we associate a lunar event with the mind, the red and orange hues of the sun directly affect shape and form—the body. When solar eclipses occur during a new moon, jungle fires increase, and the possibility of earthquakes also increases threefold. A solar eclipse causes imbalanced body temperatures in the human body. High fevers, hyperthyroidism, inflammatory infections, heat exhaustion, and cramps are a few common examples.

Yet, astrology's precision remains as it is—a mathematical equation. As Carl Jung said, 'We are born at a given moment in a given place and, like vintage years of wine, we have qualities of the year and season in which we are born. Astrology does not lay claim to anything else.'

It is important to note that all forms of astrology involve two vital aspects: The first one is theory which considers spherical geometry and movement of the planets for its calculations, and the other is the artistic ability to foretell or predict certain phenomena, events, or situations. No agencies or off-shoots of an astrological chart determine one's future journey.

Yet, astrology is an intrinsic part of communities; a deeply embedded tool, a hopeful device, an invisible authority easily accessed in South-Asian cultures and households. The importance of auspiciousness precedes any event, and therefore timing is important for any religious, cultural, and personal occasion. All for a balanced result. But astrology is also widely used as a predictive tool. We want to know the unknown. I base predictions on historical environments, cultural/social biases, and local interferences. It is the human that errs more than the calculations. In my analysis, four major conduits influence the value of forecasting. Fifty per cent of the analysis comes from a summary of calculations on a birth chart or as Jung states, 'The year and season one is born in.' The ancestry, heredities, and the culture one is born into influence the next twenty-five per cent. The last twenty-five per cent depends on the relative influences of the present—the immediate circumstance and the geographical environment at the time of birth.

Finally, intuition or the insight of the practitioner makes up for the fourth element in the analysis of a chart. Just as painters manifest their intent and insight onto the canvas, astrologers voice a reading from intuition and insight too.

Information and its effective communication are two inseparable sides of the same coin. The headline, as presented, holds the power to make or break the path of present and future thought. Communication thus turns into a responsibility, a doorway that must remain wide open to inference borne of awareness and not ignorance.

Personally, the courage to convey a thought arose through constant validation. It is what pushed me onwards and forward to explore further. When family, clients, and friends return to appreciate accuracy, I consider it a barometer for authenticity. My skill lies somewhere in between the calculation of astrology, experiential philosophy or intuition, and the ability to access the vibrations behind a thought.

Intuition arises from a conscious mind, nudging one with the subtlest clues and signs. According to Vivekananda, 'We must make the sharpest distinction between talk and intuitive experience. What we experience in the depth of the self establishes and stabilises within us. It leaves an imprint.'

I have spent decades contemplating the crescendo of an intuitive frequency. Is clairaudience a frequency? Is it related to the fact that every speck of the universe dances to a rhythm, a vibration? Do I access this moving string of resonance? Do I notice frequencies bouncing in the atmosphere just above a being? I understand now that silence intensifies an intuitive thought. A colourful—yellow and orange, gold-laced—silence. It becomes a way of processing words, comments, behaviours, and emotions. As a child, I slipped into silence naturally. It ushered in a flood of thoughts, moving from one thought to the next to a million more till I found myself at the threshold of a filtered sound, colour, and image in its deepest clarity.

※

I am not hopeless in you
the tides of time
will decide my destiny.
Wherever you may be,
you still live within me.
Each moment,
subtle feelings
grow in me,
gently, gently,
tiptoe in me,
like flowers,
bloom in me,
like a day
melting into the twilight.
I am not hopeless in you
the tides of time
will decide my destiny.

16
Through the Open Door

It was the middle of August 1991, when Shanti Golecha and I drove to the Green House in Jaipur. We were visiting a high-ranking *Svetambara muni*, Nathmal Mahapragya. Jaina monks often move residence with the changing seasons to stay at a religious teaching institute and residence situated in a different region of the country.

Jaipur is one such location during monsoons where many followers of the Jaina sect organise places of transitory existence for the *acharyas*. I encountered such ascetics of the Terapanthi traditions partly because of Shanti bhai, a close associate, client, and the acting president of the Terapanthi Samaj or society. I always wanted to meet them because the intricate yet contradictory nature of the Jaina sect's methods, concepts, and ideology, intrigued me.

In the glare of a desert's afternoon, I wore a bright fuchsia and gold bordered kota zari sari with a flame orange blouse and walked into the precinct with a sense of flourish. I tiptoed through the corridors lest I disturb the pure white spaces we crossed. Occasionally, I stopped to stare at the plainness, feeling quite appropriate in the setting; much like the relief rendered in a carafe of summer flowers with lush green stalks laying against whitewashed walls.

I waited at the threshold of Mahapragyaji's room while bhai walked over the dividing step to announce my arrival. I looked in through the open door and saw a monk pacing the room. Through the thin folds of a pure white voile *pangarini* (upper garment), I saw his slender arms clasped behind his back while he took quick strides, stretching the tight circumference of his *cholapattak* (the lower garment that touched his shins). Across India, many had heard tales of Mahapragyaji's agility and speed. He was a disciplined monk and at seventy-two, he walked faster than most from point A to a faraway point B, refusing travel by any other means. Even in this little space, I watched the nifty footwork through his pristine ankle-length socks. He glanced at me when walking close to the doorway and caught me smiling as I clocked the clumsy manoeuvres of two attendants, trying to keep pace with their leader.

Bhai asked me to enter and then gestured abruptly, telling me to stop on the other side of the threshold. I looked on as Mahapragyaji halted abruptly to face me from the far end of the room. His square-rimmed rustic gold spectacles caught my eye, and I thought they were like a crown of sorts, adorning the austere bald head, face, and pronounced tall ears. A majestic centrepiece bringing all else into focus.

He spoke through a *muhpatti* (a mouth mask), 'So, what *jati* (caste)?'

I looked at him with a steady gaze, while bringing my hands together in namaskar, 'Mahapragyaji, *maanavjati*. I am from the caste of human beings.'

He smiled, dismissing me with a wave of his right hand. 'That is not what I asked. Please answer my question. What caste?' he asked again.

'Well then, I belong to the *aurat jaat* (female class),' I said plainly.

'Jain, Sikh, Punjabi, Kshatriya, Brahmin . . . what kind?'

'Mahapragyaji, as far as I know, Jain is not a caste; it is more of a sect, a tradition, or a system followed by a community of people. I was born to Sindhi parents from the region of Sindh, in Pakistan, and I speak Sanskrit, Urdu, Hindi, and Sindhi. I am here to draw from your insight and wisdom. If you insist, I will wear a muhpatti and adopt the practice of abstinence from food after sunset to become Jain.'

An awkward silence dragged on, unhindered for more than a mile. No one interfered till I spoke again. Hands still clasped in namaskar, I asked, 'Acharyavar, so should I come in now?'

The *muni* smiled, 'Come in and do not worry. I was simply curious when I heard of your perseverance as a seeker of gyan.'

I scanned the room for something more than the blank scape. An attendant motioned to the thin mattress laid out in the far-right corner of the room. Covered with a crisp sheet neatly tucked in corners, a beam of sunlight stressed the purity of white cotton. I propped myself in the lotus position supported with a firm white bolster against the wall.

After a brief chat with the muni, one of the aides hastily scurried out of the room. Shanti bhai followed him out on the pretext of catching up with official work. The other aide stood by the door while I, the animated fuchsia distraction in a passive white environment, watched every dividing line in the room. The muni lived the concepts he advocated. Non-possession, austerity, detachment, a desire-free existence, and most of all, the *Anuvrat* movement. His initiative for a nonviolent socio-political community of self-transformed people was now a global phenomenon. As an individual, he was essentially clothed, ate food offered by householders, and walked the length and breadth of the country. I wondered why ascetics like him needed attendants at all.

The aide returned with a neatly folded envelope pouch. Mahapragyaji placed it on the white sheet where I sat.

Cautiously, I untied the golden string while a couple of tiny brass bells, attached to both its edges, tinkered in approval. The deep-toned charmeuse silk fabric felt warm against my palm. With slow deliberate movements, I unfolded four sides of triangled furrows to reveal a single folded script. Then lifting one edge of the paper carefully, I unfolded a birth chart, hand drawn in royal blue ink on an exquisite ivory and gold handmade paper. It said: *'Muni Nathmal, Vikram samvat 1977, Krishna paksh Trayodashi'* which corresponds to 14 June 1920 in the Gregorian calendar. Under this was a breathtaking hand-sketched *kundli* which is a calculative diagram drawn with specifics of time and birth detailing planets stationed at a certain degree.

The consideration for a birth chart touched me. It echoes the care and respect for a personal imprint. Yet, I could not help but observe the muni's attire. Did the body not deserve protection in the extremity of shifting sands? Why did a non-possessive monk keep a birth chart so preciously? What more was there to discover in an austere mechanical existence?

A copper penny danced on the marble-chipped floor, resounding loudly in my stomach. I was witnessing the play of double consciousness. I faced someone who walked with a defined destiny, performed repetitively every single day, and constantly contemplated one's existence. Why would a man with a dedicated life have me study his birth chart?

I wondered what the monk's questions might be. Maybe he wanted an insight into the personal journey of *nirvana* (liberation), or he wished to know of any major illness he needed precautions against. After all, he managed the organisation, and his ill health might put a lot at risk.

With reasonable order in my head, I scanned the chart. Pictures, symbols, and colours flashed in the intuitive subconscious. I looked up casually, waiting for a question.

Mahapragyaji paced the room once more before he stood closer and said in a hushed tone, 'When will I get international fame?'

I thought I had misunderstood the question.

'Acharyashri, I do not understand your question. The Anuvrat movement you have started has over a million followers in the world. Jainism affords worldwide recognition of its principles because of its logical methods, and there is a growing appreciation for its ideology.' I just could not make sense of the question. Mahapragyaji wrote a lot and that helped to spread the concepts he taught and practised. But I wondered how he could get international fame if he travelled on foot and would not sit in an airplane to claim the fame. Also, this was 1987 when Twitter and Instagram were far-stretched ideas.

He stared at me and the chart with a lopsided smile. I lingered for him to say something and sensed he was expecting elaboration. We both waited.

'Well, that's what I meant, due recognition of the sect and its principles,' Mahapragyaji finally spoke.

'Mahapragyaji, what is the relevance of a birth chart in the life of a principled ascetic? The three ethics you follow have carved your destiny. Simplicity in character lies beyond the complexities of the mind. You live in harmony every day of your life. There is no alteration in the pattern; the twenty-seven segmented lunar motions that forever orbit around causing the experiences of joy and sorrow cannot influence your destiny,' I offered.

A while later, I elaborated on his health, and we discussed when major planetary shifts may affect his movements and work. After that, we spoke of astrology through a wider lens, discussing the technical differences in astrological charts made in the south and north of India.

This was my first meeting with Mahapragyaji. I remained quiet on the journey home. I had a lot to learn. When hidden cracks appear, a lesson always reveals itself. I wrote in my journal that night, 'It is a complex situation. Ethics alone does not raise consciousness. Sanity stands on a thin wire swaying between believed ethics, historical practices, effort, and the destiny to lead a socio-religious institution. It is however a reluctant choice for preserving orchestrated traditions and in the process, sacrificing the inner resolve.'

During my interactions with Jain munis and the supporters of the sect, I observed their habits, rituals, methods, and discipline. Their pale glowing skins, soft features, dainty hands, and immaculate appearances revealed a deep sense of care and diligence. Yet, I also experienced their inhibitions, intensity, and repressions. They were some of my best teachers.

The founder of the community, Mahavira swami, introduced methods with a rational approach, focussing on the central theme of a 'principle in practice,' yet today one follows rituals without question. Mahavira denounced the intake of food after sunset with the idea derived from the principle of ahimsa that rejects the killing of another creature. As there were no bright bulbs in 599 BC, the possibility of swallowing a mosquito or a tiny insect was obvious. So, the saint's decision against eating in the dark was rational back then but people support these derelict ideas not because it may help digestion but more because of a shackled social allegiance they cannot escape.

The same logic applies to straining water before they drank it; a practice to get rid of live bacteria in water. Makes sense but nowadays, they boil the water and drink it, so they have bypassed the basic principle of not killing bacteria. Yet, for most, it is difficult to admit that such practices bear no significance to spiritual growth.

The other principle is *aparigraha*—non-possession, non-attachment, and abstinence from the rise of a desire. In the practice of this principle, Jaina monks reject all possessions, relying on householders for their frugal meals. They insist that a lighter emotional body complements a healthy elemental and intellectual self, leading to higher consciousness. This rigorous discipline is an effective tool for *samyak darshan* (the right understanding). No doubt, the munis I associated with were experts in theoretical knowledge, yet they suppressed their emotions, feelings, and the experience. They missed any spark of spontaneity. No one spoke of their personal experiences of feeling and touch. Listless words circulated in a conditioned space, all from the references of prescribed aphorisms.

I met Mahapragya again as the *yuvacharya*, the designated successor, two years before Acharya Tulsi publicly declared him the acharya, the tenth supreme head of the sangha. Initiated into monkhood at thirteen, Mahapragyaji was a keen translator, spoke four languages, and authored various books on Jaina concepts. He practised and experimented on various meditation techniques, and loved sharing his lifelong experiences condensed in the *preksha* meditation system. I looked forward to our meetings when we discussed topics of mutual interest in history, philosophy, astrology, and sociology. For years, I studied his work, *Bhaktambar Ka Antarstar* and debated with him on the higher ideals of the mind. Accessibility and evolution of Jain doctrines across the globe became his mission in life.

On another occasion, I met Mahapragyaji for a meeting to discuss auspicious dates for upcoming events. After the meeting, Golecha bhai and I walked past all the rooms in the long corridor. He then stopped by a door. Looking into a well-lit room with lofty ceilings, he stepped forward and introduced me to Mahapragyaji's teacher, the supreme head of the Swetambar Terapanth, Acharya Shri Tulsi. We both bowed to him.

'Acharya Shri, this is Nirmala. A gifted astrologer,' bhai said.

I admired his delicate, flawless, bright-eyed face as he turned to look at me. He too wore a muhpatti. Acharya Shri Tulsi waved his hand upwards, beckoning us in, but I mistook it as a gesture for me to say something.

In that one abrupt moment, I said, 'With due respect Acharya Shri, when the time comes, you will not attain what you seek. You will not gain *santhara* (methodical purification of the body before the transference of the self from one body to another).'

A shocked silence ensued. Bhai stood aghast turning hopelessly pale. In the next few minutes, two aides warned me to mind my wayward tongue.

'You forget where you stand, and we will not allow you to come back,' one man said.

I turned to face the ascetic again, 'Acharya Shri, you are an accomplished yogi with impeccable commitment to your principles. On instinct, I often predict twenty events in a day but claim no certainty. In time, this vision will claim its own truth irrespective of my words. I spoke in an intuitive moment and humbly accept my limitations as a human open to error.'

Acharya Shri stood motionless for some time, so I spoke again, 'I do not know if you are assessing my calibre, Acharya Shri. Although I profess neutral predictions, I understand you may be beyond the desire to attain anything at all. From that perspective, this prediction bears no relevance at all.'

Silence sliced through a thick cloud of trepidation. It enraged Golecha bhai. 'You have disrespected our hospitality and the honour of the Terapanthi sect. I should not have brought you here,' he said.

'Visiting the head of a sect is not the privilege of a few, as you may believe. Interactions happen for a reason much larger than our myopic perception and if destiny designs that I meet a hundred yogis, not much will come in the way. Who knows that

I may come again, and Acharya Shri may bless me next time,' I said with a smile and folded hands.

Acharya Tulsi quietly gestured for them all to disperse and walked towards the threshold of his room where I stood. He blessed me wholeheartedly. A few years later, someone from the sangha came to my office with the sad news that he died of a massive heart attack.

Nathmal Mahapragyaji took the Anuvrat movement forward from Acharya Tulsi, inspiring millions of Indians to live a life of self-restraint. A colossal effort. He walked thousands of miles to propagate the movements he believed in, and the community looked up to the celebrated monk for advice. His passion for spreading a method towards harmony and peace turned into a burden of obligation and allegiance. Over the years, I watched an intelligent mind split in half. Mahapragyaji saw the dangers too yet could not walk away. The organisation feared losing him because they were deeply invested in his intelligence and public capacities. Finally, the burdens of a socio-political obligation caught the individual awareness by the throat, strangling it to obscurity. I often questioned ideological preservation in the ever-changing face of humanity. Was it not crucial to preserve one's own sanity more than anything else?

I met him on request once again, four years after he became the head acharya. He raised concerns about someone within the organisation plotting to overthrow him. I could foresee the possibility but also understood it as a common power struggle.

'Acharya Shri, you chant the *Navaakar* mantra when you walk, sit, and contemplate. Refreshed waves of energy flow within and around your environment. The frequency of the sounds neutralises any ill-will. It is most unlikely anything may harm you.'

'You are right, yet I insist you perform a fire ceremony with mantra chanting to annihilate the intention.'

I complied because somewhere I understood his dilemma. The complex layers of a mind shift and dissolve just as clouds in a moving sky. It is what makes us human beings. I performed a purifying ceremony of fire using herbs and fresh flowers. After the ceremony, I sat with a cup of tea while looking at a stunning twilight announcing the appearance of a summer's full moon.

That evening, I walked home aware that I had just performed a fire ceremony in complete contradiction to the principles. The principle of ahimsa discourages the plucking of a flower, so as not to harm living species. That night, I wrote in my journal: 'Dualism leads to doubt and confusion, not clarity. Doubting yourself leads to destruction. Vested interests function as fuel for a settling fear. Constantly nurturing the idea of unrestrictive freedom is imperative for a fearless walk.'

※※※※※

In the early nineties, people knew me as a voice reader, intuitive healer, psychic, and professional astrologer with clients all over India. One summer afternoon, while in Jaipur, a senior member of the Jain sangha asked me to mediate with an editor for substantial coverage in a leading newspaper. I was busy that day with four hospital appointments to see clients and forgot all about it. The next day, two people came into my office and slated me for my negligence. I apologised and promised to get the article printed. But administrative staff from the sangha returned a second time, berating me for the little space the article covered. This time, I requested an audience with the religious leader alone.

'You are a woman,' they said. So, I asked for permission to speak my mind in the presence of his three aides and a senior muni. Mahapragyaji nodded, asking me to sit.

'Acharya Shri, I am here to understand this situation better. Citizens like me walk through chaos, difficulties, desires, tears, laughter, agendas, and all sorts in a day, whereas you live a perfectly organised, uncomplicated day. There is not much comparison. So, for a renunciate to seek personal value and recognition bewilders me. How does the allocated print space hold any relevance? I can understand the socio-political needs of the organisation but not the rest of it.'

The expressionless faces in the room agitated me more, and I said, 'I am no renunciate. I relish every colour life offers me. I dress well, eat well, and interact as best I can. It validates my being within a social framework. But you have restrained your senses in every conceivable way. You looked away from the fame and recognition that was yours, and you live sparingly.' I paused. Nothing changed, so I continued, 'Acharya Shri, from my position, I observe that in the practice of renunciation, you did not feel or transcend the pleasures of the sweetheart, and you stand miles away from the joys of divine grace.'

The leader did not answer, but his deputy reprimanded me, questioning whether I was there to learn and discuss or to criticise. I believe questioning is the first occupation of humanity; an important step towards further understanding. This outburst affected me. I respected Acharya Nathmal, his ideals, discipline, and insight. However, I also owe him credit for instilling the most important principle of my life—do not attach yourself permanently to anything that hampers your own growth and learning. No organisations, no foundations, no sects, and no positions of authority that borrow from ideas of control and mass followers.

After this incident, I stepped back from the public eye refusing to give interviews for the next decade. I had collected a repertoire of stories, questions, human tendencies, insights, and opinions, right from the age of seven, and now I took time to assimilate all those different perceptions in a thought. The time away helped me to understand the intricate layers of inference, meaning, and context. I realised that our explanations stem from historical, ethnic, social, and political references or personal interactions. I needed time to cope with the rampant and colossal contradictions at every step. I also realised how nourished I feel through interaction. It affords me the freedom to question, learn, and voice my opinion without fear. Silence steadies me with clarity, whereas a healthy discussion expands knowledge.

I do not agree with asceticism. One cannot escape the senses or the mind. It is like saying, I will walk without a nose to smell or with eyes closed to the splendour of changing light. Asceticism begins with a profound discipline but gradually perforates into the realms of escapism. Often, the attendants questioned my audacity, and I said, 'Look around you. This life force, your own breath, remains undivided. It is not dependent on anything. Independent, it flows. Yet, it is a powerful thread that makes each bead interdependent. You and I cannot escape it. There is no escape.'

Your identity lies far beyond my bounds.
Away from realities, it searches
for the very origin and the farthest limits.
I sense the 'I' of your identity
deep within the confines of

my body and being
within which
my longing and I
each search for our eternal void
and this unfettered search for you
carries the yearning of my sentient self
to visions where
soulful springs flow
and in all of these springs, I see
your reflection,
yours
only yours.
I realise now,
you are my dawn
you are my twilight
you are my divinity
and you
are my prayer.

17
A Blank Unknown

In the winter of 1987, I accompanied an associate to a spiritual seminar near Delhi's suburbs. The sun was just going down, while birds gathered in the trees, and a coy twilight descended in the distance. As we took our place, this friend gave me a ten-minute monologue on the required etiquette and protocol. I observed quietly.

A tall woman, in her early forties, led an audience of a thousand people. With garlands of fresh marigolds around her neck, she sat cross-legged on a raised platform. Volunteers and organisers assisted the audience to sit on red dhurries spread out on the manicured greens of a farmhouse. The lady raised her arms up, while leaning forward to place her lips close to the microphone.

Suddenly, I heard a jarring scream through the speakers, 'Close your eyes . . . now your eyes are closing. Now your *kundalini* is a-w-a-k-e-n-i-n-g . . . is awake-ning. It is awake-ning, it is a-wake-ning . . . it is now a-wakened!'

The last word 'awakened' dropped heavily on the body in a loud and abrupt demand; a finality echoing through the obnoxious speakers and crash-landing somewhere in the centre of the venue. The sounds sent a revolting shiver through my being.

I did nothing. With my arms down and eyes wide open, I took the picture in. This woman moved even closer to the mouthpiece, 'Now tell me, dear followers, who all can feel their kundalini rising?'

Shocked at the spectacle, I looked around for an entire minute, shuffling in my place. Each person in attendance raised a hand, including the client I was there with. Soon, surprise gave way to doubt. I could not resist the intense urge to question what she said. Instead of raising just my hand, I lifted myself to stand and looked around.

People began shuffling while two attendants from either side walked towards me. Steadying myself, I turned to the one on my left and raised my voice, 'Please explain the word kundalini, the thing that has just been raised in so many people. I am young and slow, but I wish to learn.'

A third person, someone from the inner circle, came from the front and gestured, ordering me to sit down and not waste time. But I stood there waiting for a response.

'Look around you.' This man waved his hand to the crowd. 'Look all around you. An awakened crowd surrounds you, young one. You have questioned it because you are not aware yet.'

Bringing my hands together in namaskar, I cleared my throat, and said, 'Yes, so true, and because this lady is the teacher, I have a straight question, so I can understand too.'

My acquaintance on the left and a stranger to the right, pulled my shirt and then my arms, forcing me to sit back down. I got no answers, but heard a thousand thoughts hurtled in my direction, all asking, 'How dare you question?'

On the way out, I commented to my disgruntled associate, 'If you asked eighty per cent of the people here what kundalini means, they will not know. Do you realise the irreversible damage such blind following causes?'

She was too defensive to listen. Speaking of this incident, I still feel a wretched despair bubble to the surface. I was twenty-two then, and my naïve heart could not understand the turmoil for weeks. The sight almost terrified me. I wrote in my diary that night: 'If I am uncertain, I must allow doubt. I must question and enquire fearlessly without the garb of decorum and politesse. Words mean nothing without efficient context, historical relevance, and evidence. I cannot trust these words. Dogmatic belief is not trust or faith. It is an effort to repress healthy doubt. Pretence breeds self-doubt, not self-confidence.'

This incident also strengthened my resolve to collaborate independently with people in a personal one-to-one relationship. No prefixes, titles, institutions, followers, or organisations where authority is misplaced or put on a pedestal. I hope I never lose the touch, feel, and sincerity of an intimate conversation where we both remain open to questions, to explore, to have a great laugh, and to share a beautiful meal.

When I listen to someone or access the vibration in a voice, I hunt for purpose, for a defining chord in the ripples. I do not administer a dose without examination. While chanting I wait to hear sounds resonate within me for as long as it takes before I register anything or consider the influence. All words emerge from a preceding thought. If I listen further than the skin of a word, I discover its intent, purpose, and sincerity in the echo. I do not get swayed away with a shout and a scream.

Neera, a friend, visited after a gap of four years and spoke of a Buddhist group she loved going to. Chanting the mantra '*Nam Myoho Renge Kyo*', she felt a strong connection within. It calmed her anxieties and fears.

The mantra, a Sino-Japanese pronunciation has travelled in transliterations from the Chinese chant, '*Miao-fa-lienhua-ching*', which originates from copied commentaries found hidden in high-walled chambers of monasteries as early as 508 AD. Buddhist monks of Takshila translated these copies in India, who chanted a similar meaning Sanskrit verse: '*Namami Reem Kleem Hyom*' around 400 AD. The words differ, but the root vibrations are similar and so is the inference. When I broke the chant down for Neera, she looked at me nervously. The explanations confused her because she sang a verse with feelings and an honest intent. She did not bother with the etymology of words.

Well, that is the point; her intent was far stronger than the actual words she was chanting. Purpose fuelled an acceptance, and in that space, the sounds resonated with her. Intent enables a driving force beyond the constraints of logic. In that moment, an unchartered frequency finds its union. So even though words dilute, a vibration remains. Thus, prayer finds its destination.

We all possess an inherent strength and deep intent. Much like a dormant seed waiting to sprout and blossom. For instance, what is a pilgrimage? What is it that makes so many people all over the world undertake journeys that are sacred, climb treacherous mountains, win races, travel a thousand miles, or feel accomplished with baking a perfect cake? Intent and awareness carry way more weight than what is correct or incorrect, right or wrong. Words follow an intent and therefore, I must be aware enough to know the purpose of what I hear and what I follow.

In my mid-forties, I met another world-acclaimed spiritual leader; a gentle, short, bearded man with a shy smile. I was excited because I believed in his achievement of bringing people together for a worldwide collective. The alliance of diverse minds and cultures brings great hope to communities and people.

A patron of the organisation requested me to visit the man with her. We went to the gathering, and she introduced me as an astrologer and a voice analyst. The guru and I both exchanged a reverent namaskar, and I sat close, watching people come for his blessings. We had a few minutes alone, and I conveyed my appreciation of his wholesome work for the progression of humanity. He laughed and raised his hand upwards, thanking grace.

Then he leaned over and said, 'Bhen, when will I get the Nobel Peace Prize?'

I composed myself, folded my hands, and replied, 'For one that bathes in the blessings of a million around him and shines in it, what is the value of a mere certificate compared to the divine fragrance around?'

The spiritual leader smiled and stared at me for a long time. I waited. The air turned stiff. He then said, 'You are so right. I asked because of all these people. It is their wish, not mine.'

That night, I wrote in my diary, 'Never doubt your own growth. Validation comes from within, not with-out. When in doubt, dive deeper into yourself to find your own confirmation, your knowing, and your integrity. Uncertainty breeds insecurity and insecurity loves the childish games of self-defence.'

Such deception claims sanity as its prize. It reveals not one but a hundred personas, all walking in different directions, disintegrated and irrational. Hypocrisy is so well wrapped in fancy ribbons that one does not see it. It is even more subtle than greed because it stems from the silent leaking of one's pretence. The drip is miniscule, not worthy of attention, but a leak persists. Hypocrisy demands pretence. A show. An act.

Certain about everything, it does not entertain doubt or self-denial. It does not suspect. It believes. It shields the mind under a comfortable canopy of acceptance. It detests disturbance. The leak persists, ultimately spilling over as a deep-seated fear, with a terrible stench of self-doubt.

Like many people of my generation, I listened to Acharya Rajneesh's Hindi lectures, fascinated with his revolutionary explanations. A Jaina rebel, he spoke slowly in chaste Hindi and broke every word down till it made sense. In one such lecture, he said, 'The mind operates within three customs. First, the ignorant, characterised by unwavering arrogance in its perpetual "I know." Second, the idiot where a slow, unresponsive brain struggles to grasp. It does not know or cares little to know. A closed door. Therefore, it shuns opportunities and turns a blind eye. The blind follower. Third, the learner, distinguished by an intelligence that continually accepts. It agrees with "I do not know" or not knowing it all and begins the long and arduous journey of endless, lifelong learning.'

During my first semester at college, a friend once shared a recorded cassette with a handwritten title, *'Diya Tale Andhera'* (Darkness under a Lamp), featuring a one-hour lecture by Acharya Rajneesh. It was the first of a series of lectures that left me thirsting for more. I found the published discourses in Hindi, with the same title in a local bookstore. I remember underlining all the lines I thought made sense. Later, I read another of his published talks, *'Kople Phir Phoot Aiyeen'* (Buds Have Blossomed Again). In fact, I read the third discourse in this book twice over, perhaps to find validation of my knowing.

I find myself recalling it more often now after the few bridges I have crossed. In this passage, the philosopher says, 'We could divide the universe into three parts: *gyaat* (the known), *agyaat* (the unknown), and *agyaya* (the unknowable). Science recognises two of the three categories: the known and the unknown. The quest of the scientific world accepts that what is unknown holds the potential that all will be known one day. But visionaries accept the third division too, the unknowable. That which was unknowable is unknowable and will remain unknowable.'

I contemplated his philosophy about the known, unknown, and unknowable. An aware consciousness connects me to the known. The ability to pick up vibrations in a voice/sound connects me to the threshold of the unknown. In a commentary on the unknown, the Upanishad scripture has a *shloka* (verse): '*Raso Ve Sah*' which translates to 'One can sense the flavour, but one cannot describe it, define it, or label it.' This statement stands true for the few who have sensed it, tasted it, or felt it but cannot define the subtlety of the unknown. Perhaps this is the knowing with which I continue to connect deeper within myself, with another human being or creature, planets, the earth, and the entire universe.

I also understand that one contends with the needs and desires of a body while in the body. Just as the Buddha, after fasting for years, one day said while sitting by the Neelanjhana river: 'Thirst and hunger are needs of the body, not a desire of the *antas* (the core).' Desire encases the elemental body in wants and therefore the body needs to quench its thirst and appease hunger. Depriving oneself of pleasures, aspirations and desires does not lead to freedom, nor will it make any difference to the intellect or to knowledge. Evolution feeds on a far deeper yearning, and not the many hungers of a body.

Yet, one process leads to the other. I like to think of the body as the most significant instrument. It encloses all aspects; the physical appearance, the sense organs, the thinking mind, the emotional bodies, the intellect, the unconscious, the unknown and possibly the unknowable. If the body, the exterior, is unsupported, its contents, struggle for support. In that context, satiety of a body's hunger allows or opens avenues to a deeper seeking of the intellect. I cannot deprive one and want the other.

I have a fragile, vulnerable yet spontaneous sense of the unknown. It is subtler than the farthest star and fleeting just like an elusive butterfly I wish to caress with my eyes a little longer, but it flits away in a hurry.

An ageing aunt became fearful and neurotic of old age and was facing its many limitations. To ease her anxious thoughts, I performed a healing yagya ceremony with mantras. I became alert and aware of her dilemma, pain, and agony. I reached out to her feelings and assured her that she would live as long as my mother. She lived even longer. This is grace. The alchemy of a force far beyond the reaches of the known world where a wish or an intuitive thought manifest.

I focus on the highest potential of an individual when I pick up one's vibrations. From conception to birth and then continuous growth, each individual gains its own unique texture and holds an experience in silence, in creativity, in organisation, and in potential. The pursuit of the highest potential of the antas (the core) lies in the acceptance of higher consciousness, not in the desire to 'become' it.

In 1984, I read an article on Acharya Rajneesh with the heading: '*Rajneesh Benaqaab*' (Rajneesh Exposed) in a local newspaper. I believed the story. The contradiction was too large for my conditioned mind. I wrote a straightforward letter to the man asking for clarification. In a few days, I received a letter from his office. It said, 'Acharya Rajneesh will reply to your question soon.' And he did in a couple of weeks.

In a small yet beautiful font, it said, 'Nirmala.' That was it. I stared at a mass of space; a blank A4 size sheet of ivory, handmade writing paper. As I ran the palm of my right hand over its fluffy texture, looking closely at the fibre bits and particles embedded in different sections, a predictable set of thoughts raced through my head. At the very bottom, on the left, in a smaller but legible size was a signature in black ink: 'Bhagwaan Rajneesh.'

A blank piece of paper has infinite possibilities. I did not know what to think, so I wrote back asking for an explanation. A fortnight later, I received another letter from Acharya Rajneesh, and it said:

'Life presents itself constantly like a blank sheet of paper.

I left the paper blank so you can fill it with your depth . . . Nirmala.

The thoughts you will fill into the paper depend on the depth of your insight.

It is up to your *buddhi* (intellect) to believe or not to believe.

To understand me, you must have a similar understanding as me.'

—Bhagwaan Rajneesh

After three decades, I understand this better. I laugh with it more. The whole incident. My reactions and his responses. Our predicaments are not much different. In the diversity of interactions, discussions, debates, and teamwork, each one stands inside a defined picture frame and understands from within those boundaries. Ironically, the picture gradually expands to become larger than its frame.

I have learnt from all the interactions I have had with monks, teachers, leaders, and the Acharya's predicament. It is another reason I avoid organised schools of thought. They create superior quality sturdy boxes which eventually box the creator in.

I met Acharya Rajneesh after his return to Koregoan. As I walked through the precinct to his private quarters, the mass display of open affection stunned my conservative foundation. Minutes later, I sat face-to-face with the Acharya. His countenance held a quietly pensive calm. Just for a fleeting moment, I sensed how he remained untouched by the influence his name carried. His eyes glowed. But then I saw a frail body almost vanishing despite the robes. I do not know why, but I asked a question.

'Acharya, do you remember I wrote you a letter?'

'Yes, Nirmala. The one I sent the blank paper to, for her to fill it with her own gyaat (knowing and acceptance),' he said in the same familiar tone as when I heard it through a cassette player.

'I understand better. A blank paper holds an unknown certainty. Pristine until a tiny drop of oil falls on it,' I said.

The Acharya glimpsed at me, and then swiftly shifted his gaze far away.

'You have walked with hope for a freedom unknown to a habituated mind whereas the likes of me live in sacrifice,' I said.

We sat a metre apart, yet he was light-years away. He said, 'So, have I not sacrificed? I wear the robes too.'

'Well, you have a beautiful ashram, you wear expensive watches,' I said.

'These define the body, not consciousness, Nirmala. Do you understand depth?' he asked.

A Blank Unknown

We met again a fortnight before his demise. For three-quarters of an hour, we sat in silence. He then arose. I saw his flowing gown all the way past his ankles. Somewhat sloppy, I thought. He was slow in his pace, and we walked to the outer room together. In our unique way, we both knew the immediate future.

This time I witnessed a paradox. I observed the eyes of a mystic and the predicament of a split personality. I wrote in my journal before I slept: 'Will I judge a book by its cover? Perhaps Osho is just an idea or, more essentially, just a wave in the ocean.'

Anything I write,
is me
talking to you for a moment or two.
Tracing you into words
adorning you on pages
is me
touching you lightly with my fingers.
Anything I write,
is me
stating my love for you.
Calling out to you with words
is me
remembering you.
Anything I write,
is me
praying for you.
My words

are not just words
they are simply
your name.

18
A Set of Brass Scales

'Nirmala, if I do not escape the urge to possess, need, and want, I risk drowning in the attraction of it all. What do you think?' Berkadia Sahib asked while we sat on a plane to Mumbai.

'There is no escape. Often, I observe myself walking a tightrope along any journey. I observe six or more personalities flare up in me from one moment to another. A theatre performance that naturally shifts as soon as a scene changes. As a counsellor, I listen and advocate. As head of the family, I decide and designate with little patience. As a sister I argue, collaborate, give, and take. In the next moment, as a friend, I laugh and share. As an aunt, I indulge, and as an involved materialistic human in a sari shop, I buy many more beautiful silks than I need. I just cannot resist such pieces of exquisite art, Berkadia Sahib.'

'That is so true, Nirmala.' He laughed.

'At times I feed the need for more knowledge, more material gains, or more peace and quiet. There is no reprieve. Wherever one travels, a new act emerges. If I became a renunciate, a new goal sets in. A spiritual hierarchy. Just as a shadow never leaves, an attraction lurks in the background constantly. Suppressing a desire is no more than fighting the elusive shadow, my dear Jiju,' I said.

Ganesh Berkadia, a noted chartered accountant in Jaipur was twenty years older than me and our association ended twenty years later when he passed on. His wife and I were close and so I addressed Mr Berkadia as Jiju, a common endearment for a brother-in-law. Jiju often accompanied me on consultancy trips to various parts of the country and we had many such conversations.

After graduation, not much had changed in my hectic routine. I was still meeting a steady stream of people for astrological consultations, predictions, and ceremonies. People came to the house and drank a customary cup of tea, while I obliged them. It was always casual with no fee for my work and services. At the time, I was also studying and experimenting with *Vastu Vidya*, the knowledge of Indian architecture in alignment with nature. The study fascinated me with its geometrical patterns, integrated symmetry, and the use of direction for a balanced flow of the elements, the sun, and moon energies in homes and workspaces. I used the study for anybody who asked but charged no one.

Indifferent to the need of a steady-paying job, I cared little for anything other than my passion to further explore hidden mysteries. Naturally, my father worried for his daughter.

'Ganesh, I am concerned for Nirmala's future. She is twenty-five years old now. Soon, my other children will marry and have support, but it is difficult for a single woman without a monthly income,' father told Ganesh Berkadia over brunch on a Sunday afternoon in 1986.

'Sewani Sahib, don't worry so much, I will talk to her. Nirmala is an intelligent girl. I will make her so resilient that our community and its people will gain from her strength.' This reassured my father.

The following Wednesday, Berkadia Sahib met me on the pretext of astrological predictions. He asked me a few questions about his business ventures, health, and so on. Ten minutes into the session, he commented, 'Nirmala, will you always remain under your parent's wings? Have you ever thought of being self-reliant and independent? Financial security enables independent decisions for both a man and a woman.'

'Father gives me monthly expenses. Three hundred rupees are enough for me and with all my other needs provided for in the family, I do not really care for money,' I replied.

'Nirmala, you are a gifted astrologer with a fast-growing clientele. A Brahmin earns more for just being able to read the almanac. Investing in a better lifestyle for yourself and your loved ones is part of sustaining fundamental ethics. Please think about this. It is important to strike a balance between the material and the ethereal or desperation creeps in. As a result, the principles we wish to preserve lose their efficacy in the ensuing struggle.'

Ganesh Berkadia clasped his hands together in a decisive clap, pushed his chair back, and stood over me. I glanced up to see him looking down through his glasses. He then turned and left swiftly, leaving the door wide open.

For over a fortnight, Jiju's words hovered over every other thought I had. It made me uncomfortable. I did not like what he said or how I defended myself. I realised I had never given much thought to earning for myself or supporting my father.

I discussed my inhibitions with both my father and Jiju in the next couple of months. I sat in my room for hours, staring at the Ganesh idol I had spoken to since I was seven. How does one charge money for something so abstract and elusive? Should I not wait till people found the evidence or their work materialised?

Jiju had an accountancy office in the centre of Jaipur. He offered me a small spare room and the use of the office telephone as well. He also decided that his receptionist would take appointments for me. The lady collected a fee of one hundred rupees for a one-hour session and gave my client a receipt.

I turned professional at twenty-five. I still met many people at home for whom one hundred rupees was a lot to pay. It did not bother me unless I heard comments about a non-Brahmin Sindhi girl going against cultural norms and the dictates of religion. Such remarks came from certain journalists and colleagues who mostly wrote to incite rather than inform.

I enjoyed this newly established structure with my work. Financial independence facilitated so much more personally, at home and among people who learnt of my intuitive abilities. Jiju's clients were business executives, my father's professional associates were from all over Rajasthan, and I knew all the jewellery specialists through the use of gem therapy. I also studied *Vaastu Shastra* and set up consultations for home and office rearrangements. Word spread mostly through verbal recommendations, attracting people from all levels of society and from various parts of the country. I started travelling to meet people for consultations and yagya ceremonies.

Yet, I did not compromise on principle. No donations. 'Earn intelligibly and win self-respect,' Jiju's advice was always at hand when scrupulous politicians and mediators approached me for favours. I was naïve but when a certain politician tried to bribe me for a favour, I threw him out of my office. I shouted so loud that the adjacent restaurant staff and all the rest came to watch the show.

I also came across those men who offered protection via foundations and institutions in my name. I refused, never conceding to pressure, monetary favours, or collaborations of any kind. It is a false garb, a fishing net. Once caught, you lose your freedom. A caged, restricted mind cannot speak or act freely. It enslaves you in hidden loyalties.

It is ironic that I encounter the occasional resentment from women too although I understand their dilemma. When women encounter one of their own on the other side of the fence, it makes them uncomfortable. They challenge my independence because it reveals their own legitimate dependency.

I have also encountered men who offer ashrams, political tickets, schools, and foundations as philanthropic gestures, but I refuse to walk under another person's umbrella. These platforms do not complement my sense of responsibility, ownership, and purpose.

In 2003, on *Vaisakh Poornima* (a full moon night) in May, a close friend and client organised an outdoor communal yagya with fifty-one *vedis* (small platforms for fire rituals) at the Hari Sharanam Ashram in Haridwar. Each platform accommodated four to five people while I conducted a mahayagya ceremony with a large gathering of four hundred participants.

The ashram's guru, Swami Ganga Das Udaseen, invited several colleagues and friends, introducing me to each one after the yagya.

One of the colleagues approached me and asked, 'Do you know who I am?'

'Yes,' I said.

'I am the one who has made one disciple a famous name today. Do you know that young woman?'

'Okay and?' I asked.

'I see you are far more intelligent than him. You have the potential to influence millions of people. I can make you even bigger than him. Look where he is today.'

'I make a decent living sir and have matured a little too. If I wanted to be like your famous student, I would not need your help. Such shops do not attract me. I am content with my work and independence,' I said.

'Such an attitude will get you nowhere. You are vain and that will not take you far in life,' he retorted.

'I did not know the man would cross his limits. Please forgive me,' Swami Ganga Dass said later.

'You need not worry. I can speak for myself. I remain conscious of such manipulative ways that undermine a woman's intelligence. I will go far. I am rooted in my consciousness, just like a great Banyan tree that spreads like a forest rather than an individual tree. What is important is that I remain vigilant so that my core and its progress are not dependent on an external attraction,' I said.

I walk free as much as possible. Staying alert and self-confident, I never sway with the winds. When caught in sticky situations, the guidance, and support from Jiju and my father always helped. I miss them when making business decisions. Jiju taught me all the numbers I needed to know. He accompanied me to all corners of the country, while I visited offices and homes for Vaastu consultations and performing yagya ceremonies. He often used my contacts as exposure for his accountancy business.

I am grateful for my association with Jiju. We were intellectually like-minded. It nourished both of us. I learnt how resources facilitate growth. Earning enough money opened doors for me to support those I could. Turning professional also put immense value to my work. I earned credibility, security, and reasonable respect in a profession barred for women. One cannot forget the inner precincts of 'goddess' temples still remain barred for her own form—women.

Constant attentiveness kept me grounded in reality. I remember, Yogesh Mishra had a beautiful set of miniature brass scales with tiny weights, which sat in the centre of his bookshelf. I loved playing with them as a teenager. Much later I understood his insight and why he loved them as a constant reminder.

Untouched, a set of scales holds a crucial key—balance. Place the slightest weight onto a brass plate. Whichever way it tips, left or right, scales lose balance instantly. I realised the need to balance my outer and inner self, matter and energy, to find an integrated stability between the two. Any principle is personal to each of us. We may imbibe it from gurus and teachers, but the effort is solely individual. I walked ahead, constantly keeping a keen eye on my aim—to facilitate internal expansion through external growth, A healthy economic flow became a means to a better lifestyle both for my family and me. It took away the burden. I was not struggling anymore, and this gradually created more space for spiritual growth. I could afford to give myself time rather than worry about the next meal, rent, and so on.

I also understood the importance of economic independence for women. It is a means of social equality with men. All my sisters are financially independent, and it changed their situation at home to a more equal footing. I especially encourage a woman, whether rich or poor, to believe in her strength and equality with men, to educate herself, and to work for her social, financial, and emotional independence.

'Nirmala, you are so indifferent towards professional growth. You do not advertise, and yet your list has grown a hundredfold since I've known you,' Jiju said one evening.

I thought about our dispositions before replying, 'Jiju, the material world offers three distinct paths. The first is self-fulfilment. Enjoying and experiencing the pleasure and pain of it all. The path of giving, contributing, and supporting, comes second but with a condition. One must support without an expectation, reciprocation, or a hidden agenda. Mind you, the first is easy while the second mostly ends in hypocrisy, but both are symbiotic options to share, distribute, accumulate, desire, or want more. These are two rational choices in the cyclic flow of matter. Because if we do not allow a flow, there is an inevitable third path: a gradual destruction of the material. Matter dissipates or stagnates in this material world. It needs regeneration. Just as a human body does; birth, growth, decay, and back to renewal.'

I benefit from both the first and the second aspects, allowing a constant flow between taking and giving. Amma always said, 'Earn gracefully with your right hand and give ever so quietly with your left. Let no one know. Keep it flowing.'

'Nirmala, you know I support my family too and give as much as I can. Yet, the effort to sustain wealth remains a task,' said Jiju.

'Well, one cannot confuse an offering with charity and so-called causes that fuel a sense of self-gratification. The moment one gives with a sense of self-satisfaction, the offering ends. It is a charitable web woven with complexities. The feel-good syndrome.

'An offering begins when the sense of ownership ends, and grace descends into the sharing. Like the sun that gives and gives and gives, silently. If wealth flows, it just flows like a nameless stretch of water. Movement becomes its sole purpose. It leaves behind the tags: who, what, why, and when. The love of giving flows in silence with no attached label. It generously multiplies and affects generations,' I said.

Berkadia Sahib contemplated for the rest of the journey, and I caught up on precious sleep. And that is another story. I travel so much between cities, I use the time for power naps in cars, taxis, trains, and planes. When I meet the client on the other end, I am ready to step into their worlds to laugh, share, work and reciprocate. The more I share without reservations, the more I grow in wealth, maturity, and respect, thus shining in the collective expansion of love.

I met Jiju three months before he passed in 2010. 'Nirmala, you've travelled far ahead of me,' he said. A lot happened in our twenty-year association. I had an office and a home in Gurgaon, and two offices in Jaipur. I travelled independently. I was far more realistic about the world and less outspoken. I assumed that was what he meant.

We met again after a week for a cup of tea and a chat. I observed his lost, vacant eyes. He spoke slowly. 'Nirmala, I know your consultation practice is three times more in value than mine.'

His words stunned me. For the last four years, I had not disclosed my financial standing to him. He figured things out for himself. There was no comparison in the practices of accountancy and esoteric consultations. I did not realise he weighed wealth as only a financial benefit.

In that moment, I accepted how different our perceptions can be even as the closest associates. I realised how it is impossible to change a thought pattern and how the mind dwells in preconceived ideas and assumptions of another's mind and thoughts. I learnt so much from his words. Although we discussed larger contributions, mobility of wealth, potential investment, and philosophy, he remained stuck in the materialistic grind. For many like him, the concept of 'work' realises and satisfies only in net profit, whereas in reality, work, is an action, any action well placed or appropriately balanced. Material benefit follows action.

That night I wrote with a heavy heart: 'Question every moment—weigh profit and loss, its importance, all its aspects and assess what path holds more value in the larger picture. An instrument or a medium has a purpose—a means to anything; to conveying, to achieving, or to completing. A medium is not the end. Thus, money cannot be the aim; that being a delusional idea.'

Berkadia sahib died a week later from a sudden heart attack. It broke my heart, leaving me aimless for a while but he also gave me the keys to prosper and thrive in a material world. I miss his hearty laugh and worldly advice.

Whichever way I look at it, financial growth allowed me to share with my siblings and others around me. Yet, any principle demands a certain discipline. I look at discipline as a personal, individual, intimate programme, because as a forced, influenced perpetuation, it ends in lost rebellion. Confused and entangled. Therefore, I must own responsibility for the inherent density of my mind. I critique and scrutinise all the information I come across and then I set my ethic, making it a discipline.

In the philosophical world, one may argue this planet is an illusion, yet existence binds everyone and everything. This existence, this survival instinct creates a desire, a want, and a longing—to exist. It is a paradox that after attaining nirvana, the zenith of wisdom and subtle understanding, the Buddha too wished for his teachings to spread far and wide. If we exist, existence binds us on this earth. The sooner I accept this reality, the more vigilant I can be and shift my discipline relatively. It allows me to distance myself further from a conditioned framework to move towards a finer, egalitarian humanity. It affords me the freedom to imagine myself as less separate and more interwoven in the fabric of existence. With this sense of adaptability, I may propose to offer more rather than grab more. In time, a deep-rooted hypocrisy may loosen its grip, making way for a fluid existence.

Through my silences, I strain to hear the force behind every attraction and interaction. I stretch my hand out to give and you take my hand to receive. A give and a take. A reciprocation. A flow. A window opens. Two hearts meet—yours and mine. My relationships, staff, acquaintances, and clients have all enriched me. I encounter all of humanity in my day—laughter, tears, growth, struggle, manipulations, corruption, and prosperity. I call this the abundance of wealth and life.

Yet, I cannot remain naïve. It is a bargain. Father supported my passion for the world of astrology and the occult. It suited my needs, my quest, and my passion. In time, I supported him too. It suited him. The attraction was mutual. Even though he was a man of principles, he took his closest relationships for granted, sacrificing his wife and me for the rest of his family.

I am often amazed at how he missed that picture. Even though I needed help with understanding science at high school, he refused to pay the tuition fees for extra help. I failed the exam. He sold my mother's jewellery so he could help his siblings settle. His reasoning—a just sacrifice, as she was his wife.

I call this partial scanning. It is the role of a father and a husband in contention with that of a brother and a man who takes pride in being the provider. His principles split at convenience to suit the alter personality. When my father refused me one hundred rupees for tuition fees and instead spent twelve hundred on his brother's family, I argued it was illogical. It did not go down well with either of us. I did not take pocket money for a while after that. Much later at university, my father offered again, and I accepted three hundred rupees every month from him as a blessing. I never used the money but collected it in a tin. Now, years after my father died, I take the box out when I miss him and touch the old notes. I feel the continuity of time.

While working at Berkadia Sahib's office, I shared the counselling fees of one hundred rupees with him. A fair deal as it was his place and contributed towards expenses. Yet, as an endorsement of protection, he accompanied me at the client's expense, marketing his accountancy interests too. A give and a take.

I gradually witnessed partnerships, interactions, associations, friendships, benevolence, and gratitude, all masking a temporary interchange. With scepticism at its dastardly best, I turned into a monstrous, disbelieving maniac out to question the legitimacy of everything. However, somewhere this atrocity became my armour, and I learnt to look at its deeper functionality. I observed the beauty and the joy in the exchange; the sharing, laughter, and learning along the journey, the tears, the turmoil of association, the uncertainty, and the vulnerability of a connection. I marvel at this phenomenon—existence binds everything.

Berkadia sahib, his wife, and I often visited a temple in Barmer, Rajasthan. On my first visit, when I was twenty-eight, I watched an auction for every activity held in the temple, from the daily bathing of the idol, its decoration, morning rituals, the evening rituals to the mass feeding of devotees. Jiju explained that a bid for a thousand rupees multiplies by four when assigned to the bidder. Bidding amounts vary per activity, with the highest bids placed for the deity rituals and feeding of the thousands that braved the queues every day.

I stood there, horrified, and could not ignore the impudence with which faith is manipulated. This was a corrupt transaction driven by power. Did people think such practices would absolve them of their guilt and fears? Worse are the torchbearers of religious sects, the priests, and the teachers who turn a blind eye to such absurdity.

In the next two hours, I watched people line up for a decent meal and a blanket for the cold evening ahead. In that relief, I almost forgave the ostentatious ways of the temple authorities in generating the needed funds. Yes, it feeds hundreds of people, and yes, it maintains the institution, its employees, and volunteers, but was it worth the mind-washing?

That night I lay on my bed, staring at the ceiling for hours. A fan whirring clockwise; round and round and round. No change in direction. I had flashes of the many cycles of friendships, relationships, interactions, and collectives, all sustained in a precious give and take, a complicit programme. Matter and attraction. A super glue with a clear agenda—it binds well. I questioned the efficiency of my principle, discipline, and existence within this bundle of contradictions. I still do.

I wrote in my journal the next morning: 'It trickles down to what I put my attention to—what I feed. That is the efficiency of the principle. In examining my motivations carefully, I must move forward with acceptance.'

Since then, I often support an individual or a collective as a nestling idea. Once it develops the wings to fly, I let go. In doing so, the support is mutual, and I keep away from any motivated attachment, investment, or dependency.

Somewhere along the years, this transaction turned into a natural process, detaching itself from a personal agenda. I refrain from the outward projection of sharing. A continuous principle in all of nature. The sun gives. The moon gives. Trees give, bees give, flowers give, and rivers give. A common being benefits.

Do the winds advertise their worth ever? Or does rain choose its destination through colour, creed, and caste? Does Mother Earth ever pull the plug on this abundant offering? She gives, and she gives. I close my eyes and listen. I hear her heart beating in the far distance as she echoes in my whispers. I close my eyes and listen again.

Today
when you come up on the open terrace
I'll turn into a kite and fly close to you.
Do caress me before I fly away
when darkness falls, I will not see you.
Today
when you come up on the open terrace
you hold the strings while I
wave in the blue sky
do not let go of me
knowingly or unknowingly
if you let go, I cannot return.
Today
when you come up on the open terrace
mind using a tight string, one impossible to snap
pull me towards you when
the other tries to snatch me.
Today
when you come up on the open terrace.

19

The Hidden Womb

I hear the incessant chatter of birds with the faint awareness of dawn. I wonder where I am. I do not know what realm the birds are in. With the two precious curtains still drawn over my eyes, I take a deep breath and compile images from the night in one more memory capsule.

I sense my surroundings. In the distance, I hear grating calls of what I think is a long-tailed shrike. The sound shifts from that of a cuckoo to a lapwing and then to the urgent squealing of a frog caught by a snake. I marvel at how intelligent sound is. This bird can mimic several sounds and its ability to sing makes it a common pet for bird lovers in Rajasthan.

The crooning turns sharper forcing me to open my eyelids and jump out of bed. I run to the window on my right to catch one sharp glimpse of a peach-breasted bird. It takes off in a hurry, leaving me in awe of this tiny glimpse of a magnificent creation. The ordinary attracts my attention more than anything. Sounds, smell, touch, and feel are all a common familiarity driving my day. Between counselling, healing ceremonies, and travelling for hours on end, I have responsibilities too like most people. The habit of a mechanical day catches up with me too and I have little patience for the imperfect and the complacent. Beeping horns and traffic annoy me.

At thirteen, I read Swami Vivekanand's words from the six lessons of Raj Yog and often began my morning with his lines: 'Fasten the mind to one idea. Take that idea/subject before you and think it through; never leave it. Do not count time.'

Most humans constantly search for an individual purpose. Some fix their thoughts on a desired discipline or study till they find a purpose. Often the desire shifts mid-way. Many fasten the mind through constant action; any physical work where the hands, brain, and mind are busy with a fixed task. A few find immense purpose in service. Helping or caring for others removes the mind's focus on the 'I', shifting it to the other as the subject. For a while, the personal recedes into the background. Yet, whichever way one chooses, the process is gradual. As the mind steadies itself, one walks the bridge from the individual to a collective purpose.

'Fasten the mind to one idea.' I found my way through the constant search for gyan, a Sanskrit term that has no synonym in spoken English. It closely amounts to the hidden knowledge of wisdom and insight. Growing up in my busy environment, I sped through it all, always in a hurry to cover time. My mind moved faster than itself, almost forgetting to stop and admire the flowers by the side of the road. The finishing line was always far too bold. The finer, more delicate, ordinary moments receded into the distant background just as the lines in the palm of one's hands. We do not have the time to look at them. They carve their permanence in the most ordinary manner, yet they are profound.

At twelve, when I fasted, remaining silent for thirty-five-hour stretches, I never thought what it may entail for my mother. I could not see the difficulty of a mother who constantly watched her child starving. In running a race from the start line to the chequered flag, I battled with what was in between—the colours, fragrances, emotions, potholes, and relationships.

In time, I slowed down enough to stop, wait, and listen because I realised that the journey is not an illusion. When a mother sees her child running into a wall, she will either pull the child away or somehow block the collision by dragging, slapping, or shouting at the child to divert attention. In that moment, there is no science, no logic, no boundaries, no limits, and no established principle involved—just pure instinct. An ordinary moment; personal, spontaneous, and connected.

I gradually learnt to bend down and touch flowers, feel the thorns, pick up the pebbles, allow the sounds of heavy rain to disturb my peace, and count stars without wanting to know their names, all of this while my mind remains fastened to one focus: to dive deeper into the ocean for a better understanding. Therefore, I need a discipline. An internal and external restraint. It dispels anxiety. It also turns into a habit.

My father died when I was thirty-three, and I accepted more work. I travelled all over the country to meet clients, interacting with people constantly, performing yagya ceremonies and consulting with their families. I looked forward to staying with people in their homes and sharing good food. I met many people in the west of India. Among them, an eminent personality, Raja Sahib, came to trust my abilities and expertise. He appreciated my quest for knowledge and admired the ingenuity behind mantra invocation and ritual. We often discussed complex philosophical concepts and texts on Indian spiritual ideology.

'Nirmala bhen, you are a *sadhika*; an earnest disciple of life and its mysteries, not just an *aradhika* (a devotee),' he said. On one such appointment at his office in June 2004, Raja Sahib introduced me to the religious head of Mumbai Mahalakshmi temple. We exchanged pleasantries, and I realised that he was there to discuss ongoing temple ceremonies for the re-consecration of the inner sanctums. The inner sanctum of India's ancient temples holds fossils as old as the subcontinent itself. These fossils are impressions of living entities, much like wombs, emanating forceful energies. In India, millions of devotees enable the preservation of these forces through the power of their intent and devotion. It is this collective intent, an undying hope in the unknown that makes any place of worship a powerful sanctuary.

Anyhow, ten minutes into the discussion, I observed Raja Sahib pacing the room, deep in his thoughts. He paused, turning to face the man who stood up on cue. 'Nirmala will perform the consecration of the inner sanctum, the *garbh* (womb), Shankaracharyaji. Please assist her with the ceremony.'

Pin drop silence. I watched the head priest step back, shuffle, and tweak his shawl that sat in immaculate folds over his shoulder. It was an awkward moment. I did not know if I should stand up, so I remained seated.

'Raja Sahib, I thought the ceremony was just for the idol consecration, the *stupas,* and not for the *garbh pratishthan* (the womb or the fossil). More importantly, I am sure you know women cannot enter the inner sanctum or perform such sacred ceremonies.'

'Where did you read that Shankaracharyaji?' I asked, standing up quickly to face the men.

'In the *shaastras* (the sacred texts), and as responsible leaders, it becomes our duty to uphold *parampara* (traditions),' Shankaracharyaji said, while tweaking his shawl with immense authority this time.

This is the one careless statement that challenges every nerve of patience within me. 'Our duty to uphold traditions is mutual although my responsibility also demands constant speculation. In all of my study of the scriptures, I have not encountered what you just said, Acharyavar.'

'Then you have not read enough Nirmala bhen, or you choose not to,' the priest said.

'Acharyavar, if one researches far back into the Sanskrit texts around 500 BCE on the *Sattvic yug*, the wives and daughters of the rishis were equal participants in all yagya ceremonies. I refer to *Gargi, Maitriya,* and *Lopa mudra*. But, through the last ten centuries, an exclusive class of men have continuously censored the liberties of women like me with diluted interpretations of Sanskrit 'shaastras' to maintain a patriarchal hierarchy. Obviously, along the way, I have missed all relevant verses on such divisive instructions, so please educate me. A healthy debate expands understanding and the evolution of the common being,' I said.

Silence contradicted its own purpose in that moment, crashing down like broken glass. I watched Raja Sahib pacing the room, saying nothing. I spoke again, pointing a finger at myself, 'And now Acharyavar, in this provocation, I, a woman, will re-write my own interpretations and eliminate the self-centred, unyielding male brigade from it.'

Raja Sahib laughed aloud, amused at my outburst. He recovered quickly as he sensed the dilemma. In an attempt to resolve the issue, he spoke in the tones of a seasoned soft-spoken authority. 'Shankaracharyaji, I have known Nirmala for a while now and am convinced of her capacity and capability for the job. Please perform your part of the ceremony and she will address her part.'

Looking into the priest's eyes, Raja Sahib added, 'And if it does not convince you to perform the ceremony of the stupa, I am sure Nirmala will gladly step in for that too.' Few dared to speak when Raja Sahib spoke in that tone. A shaken priest stood there in disbelief, baffled, and betrayed by a member of his own clan—the man. He could not understand.

A new silence followed. One that felt uncertain of its own relevance as the seconds ticked away louder and louder. The priest turned to face me. He said nothing for a while, yet I heard it all. 'So, how do you intend to perform this ceremony? Alone? Where are the rest of the pundits? Did they come with you from Jaipur?' he questioned quickly, looking over my shoulder with mocking eyes.

'Hukum,' I addressed him with folded hands, speaking slowly, 'I will perform this ceremony on my own.'

'Really? Do you know it takes a good four to five hours for this ritual?'

'I am aware, and if I get stuck at any point hukum, I am sure you and your team of seventeen men will assist me in the auspicious completion of this grand service.'

The ground shifted from under the man's feet as he skipped two steps backwards, bumping into the wall behind him. So far, he had not disclosed to either Raja Sahib or me, about his preparation or the number of assistants he planned to deploy for the ceremony. The *Shankaracharya's* expressions changed. He moved quickly, pulling back at least an ounce of the initial resentment. Intrigue stepped in and he now wondered how I had accessed the information he had revealed to no one.

The following morning, I wore a mustard, gold, and moss green pure silk, *Kanjeevaram* sari with pearl ear drops. I entered the inner sanctums of the temple, carrying flowers in four colours—white, red, yellow, and pink. Gazing at the dark walls of the small cave-like ancient space, I wondered how old it was and how many women had been there before me. The people who took care of the temple had neatly lined up everything I asked for; three distinct kinds of wood, spices, herbs, sweets, and fruits. I sat cross-legged, placed the flowers on an empty brass tray and lit the *dhoop* (a smoky, thick, hand-rolled incense). After a deep breath, I let out a slow exhale in gratitude for the opportunity. The mixed fragrances of chameli (more Gardenia than Jasmine), rose, and herbed incense, all infused upwards in circles. I closed my eyes and thought of

Ganesh; the one who brings me to an auspicious threshold. Hitting a sublime space, I chanted for hours on end. The idol of the feminine, the sounds, the rhythm, focus, intent, and an intimate feeling for a mother, all reverberated in unison. Nothing stood separate.

After five hours, I completed the sacred ceremony of *garbh pratishthan pratisthapana*, reinstating, replenishing, and renewing the sacred womb in the innermost sanctum of the Mahalakshmi temple. Offering the last prayers, I bowed in reverence, first to the divine feminine and the primordial womb, then to the profundity in gyan—creative knowledge, understanding, wisdom, and insight, and lastly to the few people sitting in the small sanctuary.

The smoke from the dhoop quietly tiptoed around a soft space, almost like it did not want to intrude. Pure space. Light yet steady. A precious moment when a woman honours her own essence; the primordial mother and her womb. For a moment, I melted into the flame, emerging slowly, renewed, redefined, and rekindled. The few people present bowed to the splendour of honour and unity. I looked over at Shankaracharyaji seated in the lotus position, motionless. Tears streamed down his cheeks just like the spontaneity of an artesian spring so oblivious to its surroundings. Pure instinct of an emotional being.

We sat there quietly till someone stepped in with tea. After we ate *prasaad*, a more composed Shankaracharyaji nodded his head and spoke a few words.

'Where did you learn this, bai?'

I folded my hands and said, 'Through the grace of my guru, Acharyavar.'

'Bai, I was thirteen when I took *diksha*. Since that day, I have performed five ceremonies daily, at dawn and sunset. Yet *siddhita* (the awareness or preservation of subtle energies) eludes my being. The responsibilities of the organisation are heavy and have side-tracked my initial focus in the quest for wisdom.'

I nodded. The Shankaracharya had dropped his cloak. I saw the human.

'I empathise with your position Acharyavar. Through observing a few others of similar stature, I remained independent of such constraints and socio-religious organisations do not offer any such platforms to a woman. I have walked too many years in silence, observing misconstrued divisions in the name of protecting parampara (socially acceptable tradition). Its contradictory manifesto poses a challenge even for the most knowledgeable. But evidence speaks far more than empty words. I hope you find a renewed testimony in the demonstration of today. The feminine you worship five times a day rejoices in me constantly as a woman,' I said with folded hands. I also thanked Raja Sahib for his trust in knowledge.

Later that evening, I slept quietly on a plane back to Jaipur. A reformed silence pervaded my being. I felt accomplished. I learnt through the experience and made more notes: 'Tests and trials become stronger as one walks the narrow path. As desires continue to cloud the mind, security turns into an external commodity. As a result, even a steady secure mind collapses to the apparent hypocrisy and finally succumbs.'

I got home late and when my tired body touched the soft pillows I had another thought—the depth of my gyan (knowing), is my security. One day, it will alter and reshape this tradition, buried in the trenches of bull-headed masculinity, to redefine a woman, her intuition, her knowing, and her gyan.

A tiny bud
blooms amid thorns
yet sprinkles her fragrance
wherever she goes
never caught in the web of whirls.
Tiny she was, yet never afraid.
Her beauty, like untouched pollen
her mind, pure as sandalwood.
A tiny bud
blooms into a flower.
A tiny bud.
That is you.

20

The Dividing Line

The practice of silence grounds me and washes away any hesitations I pick up in the day. I do not doubt my breath or my being. If I find myself nervous, especially at airports, I gently touch the tip of my thumb to the tips of all four fingers in a cyclic convention. The sensations I feel bring back a sense of balance and composure. I feel steady. This is also because our fingertips possess the second-highest concentration of touch receptors making them extremely sensitive to texture, temperature, vibration, pressure, and dynamic (in motion) touch.

With relative stability, I find no hesitation in diving for treasures under the surface. We cannot know what lies deep down unless we dive for it, repeatedly. Often many flounder, doubt, divert, or lose faith in this personal quest for both the inner and outer, because of a hundred different fears. Yet, sharing one's experiences is often a means to rekindle a spark in those who may suddenly desire a knowing, walk a different path, or feel passionately for the unknown.

Ultimately, it is the choices we make. A decision to follow the intent or wait timelessly for tomorrow. At the age of nineteen, I dived deeper into the nuances of ritual. After chanting mantras for ten hours a day, I completed nine hundred and twenty-six rounds of a one hundred and eight seeded mala and strengthened the chants with a fire ceremony. It lifted my being and on one occasion, I felt myself wrapped in layers of crimson, emerald, amber, and saffron; the hues of the earth and the sky at dawn or dusk. The time in between. My body dived into a contradiction of emotions. An urgency similar to that of roaring flames flared within me in one abrupt moment and in the next moment, I dipped into swirling waves subtler than the faintest fragrances of the *parijatham* (night jasmine flowers). It is an uncertain depth. My body, mind, and senses aligned in a charged atmosphere, like being thinly encased in a golden globe sparkling in the whiteness of snow. I invoked the primordial feminine, and in the next few moments, I envisioned flashing figures in alternating hues—garish and soft. Feminine forms danced before me, within me, and around me. An intensive creative force overwhelmed my being. During this intoxicating, intense and vivid frenzy, the subtle knowledge of 'Sri' (the primordial feminine) absorbed me whole. A force began enlivening my being, bringing it to a state of *Sri siddhi*, complete surrender to an unknown feminine source. A power which nourished my being just like the roots that ground, nourish and protect a tree; roots mostly invisible to the leaves, branches, and fruit of the same tree.

In Sanskrit 'Sri' stands for prosperity abundance and wealth in all of nature's lavishness. 'Sri' also represents the mother of strength and will, the mother of knowledge and the mother of action. All three form the primordial mother in cosmic harmony. The fourth aspect draws my attention in particular. The aspect of destruction and necessary renewal. 'Sri' also forms the agency which neutralises all that is manifest, into pure existence. The entire known universe in its creation, growth, and movement, leading to its destruction and renewed evolution makes up for a life force that sustains the known universe.

For the next decade, I shape-shifted between a mundane and pristine existence. Performing various yagyas, I explored a variety of combinations in pace, rhythm, ratio, and proportion of frequencies in the atmosphere. By the age of twenty-nine, I categorised such fire ceremonies into sixty-seven combinations of healing yagyas. Each one has evolved as a signature creation for a larger objective. Each holds a unique equation or formula, that I use in permutations to suit a specific purpose. Through these keys, the primordial feminine has enabled many beings in their predicaments.

Another afternoon, on finishing one hundred and twenty-five rounds of the mala, I performed a yagya in a deeply sensitive state. Forms appeared in the flames as manifested images, and I saw flashes of a familiar feminine force in ruby-red and jade. It was familiar, but this time, I felt something more intense. I felt sharp pulsations while also seeing bursts of a silvery white and shocking gold form of light dancing within and around me. The pulsations felt much like an excruciating throb but without the pain. Then a mist of white light enveloped my body. I felt exquisite, like cloaked in a soft feathery white cushion while a flowing white light emanated from within to the outside.

I shifted my body slightly in that moment. The feeling persisted and a faint antique gold overtone seeped into the white. This white haze laced with a warm golden hue grew brighter. I cannot tell time or space or how long this feeling lasted, but I felt a tenderness and a tingling; like the aftermath of a strong wind that rakes up every leaf leaving behind the raw earth.

Subconscious, subtle, and soft experiences often leave a bold impression. They do not fade away like memories of the past. Weeks later, while walking around the Albert Hall Museum with a guest, I stopped to look at exquisite hand-painted pictures from the 6th century. One image was of a delicate, slender, and elegant feminine deity dressed in white and gold. This beautiful figure was seated in the centre of a pink lotus. In the faint handwritten description, it said—*Jain deity; Padmavati, Sasandevi Yakshini.* For a while, I stayed staring at this picture through the glass-covered panels. I could not look away when suddenly a tingling sensation ran through my body. The chattering, shuffling and movement in the small display room receded. I felt the image, the drawings, the familiar white and gold gradually mesh with my experience of a fortnight ago.

Then on, I naturally began searching specific mantras for demi-spirits (*Yaksha Vidya*) in Jain ritual texts but found nothing. I continued chanting the same mantras to awaken this force within me, trying for more than a year with no noteworthy results. I discussed the knowledge of yakshinis with many visiting seekers in the Jain community. Finally, one acquaintance from the Jain Digamber sect commented, 'Nirmala, establishing the mantra involves the tantric invocation of 'Padmavati' which are *Yakshya* (nature spirits or demigods). For this, you will have to approach certain Jain ascetics because they hold hidden keys for the realisation of Yakshya.'

Thus, a new search began and after much deliberation, I met Vimal Sagar Maharaj, an eighty-seven-year-old Jain ascetic of the high order. It was an honour to meet him. He treated me as one student would treat another but declined any knowledge of the tantric methodology. After a warm blessing, he directed me to Vidya Sagar Maharaj.

It took another year till I met the muni who questioned my reasons for the inquiry into Yakshya Vidya. We discussed tantra concepts in relation to all actions performed without personal motives. He also spoke of the differences between the two Jain sects, explaining that he was a Shvetambra Jain ascetic and ritualistic study was not his concern. He then touched my head with the palm of his thin, soft hand, saying, 'Visit a Digambar

Jain ascetic. I will let him know of the purpose. He has complete access to Yakshya Vidya.' It took a further year and a half to meet Vidyanand Muni, another ascetic of the Jaina traditions.

I walked behind an attendant through dimly lit corridors on my first visit to Dadavadi Dharamsala, Indore, Madhya Pradesh, in the heart of India. While looking into open doors on either side, I heard young student monks shuffling as they stretched to see something other than the righteous white dress code. In the exciting countdown to a new discovery, I wore an extravagant *ghagra* in lime green and Jaffa orange. I knew it was the bright yellow odhni swaying under my knee-length plaited hair that caught their attention as I flitted past each door.

Inquisitive male attendants questioned me, 'Do you know anything about our munis? Do you understand the concepts and principles of Digambar munis? You are incredibly young and as a woman do you know your limitations? Do you know how valuable time is?' It amused me. I had disrupted the order.

A quarter of an hour later, one aide guided me into a small room. I sat on the one wicker chair by the far end of an empty room. I could see a tall tree through an old wooden framed window next to the chair. Fading pictures of serious-looking, sky-clad saints, hung lopsided on the whitewashed walls. The frames were a dull orangish gold, arranged in a peculiar off-centred way on either side of the walls. Plain and careless, I thought looking back out of the open window to feel a refreshing flow of air. It relaxed my breath.

Five minutes later, three young students entered with a thin mattress and then spread it right at the threshold of the door. One of them beckoned me to sit after covering the mattress with a starched white sheet.

'It is best if you sit in such a way that you may see directly opposite through the door of the next room and into a third room. Do you understand?' he asked, pointing to where I needed to look. I shifted about for a better view. 'Please try not to move at all,' he added. I focused on the third door and could now see the austere frame of a male ascetic seated in the lotus posture. Thank goodness, for the natural light seeping in through all the windows.

With a bare room and three doors between us, Vidyanand muni sat cross-legged, about fifty feet away on a *takht* (low, long wooden bench). I folded my hands in namaskar, as he lifted his head to face me. While waiting impatiently for an invitation to go into his room, I shuffled slightly. It had been two years of waiting to meet someone who could show me the way to Yakshya Vidya—knowledge of the earth spirits. So close yet so distant. I fidgeted again.

Ten minutes later, I asked the attendant if I could go in. He said, 'As a practising Jain ascetic, it is against the principles of the sect for a woman to be in the same room as Acharyashri. Thus, the distance.' Even though I heard a storm rumbling in me, I took a deep breath, calming every single nerve bouncing for attention. Silence.

I paid attention to the relay. One attendant was in the saint's room, the second sat in the middle room, and the third attendant sat in between the second man and me. The many doors in between stood like the wooden framework of a world steeped in separation. For once I could find no excuse to separate myself from this spectacle.

I struggled to meet the monk's gaze yet held the palms of my hands together. 'Namaskar, Acharya. Thank you for your presence and time. Acharya Vidyasagar sent me here to study under your guidance,' I said. The words ambled one step at a time from the first to the fourth like a cartoon clip in slow motion. I barely saw the saint nodding to the last man in the trail. It felt like an incredible feat.

'Namaskar. Welcome. I heard of your eagerness as a seeker and will help, if possible,' these words were conveyed by the last mediator sitting near me as I strained to hear the saint's voice.

'I have come here for hidden knowledge—the mantras of Yakshya Vidya, so I may know their depth through effort and sadhana (intent).'

'Yes, please come tomorrow after the morning rituals,' I heard a voice.

The next afternoon, I arrived an hour earlier and urged the attendants, one by one, to allow me a closer view. I told them it was crucial for the teaching that I hear the muni's words for myself. Finally, I crossed the second threshold and had a better view.

After the customary namaskar, I said, 'Before we begin Acharyavar, may I ask a question?'

'Yes, you may.' I saw the saint's lips move, and heard him softly, though the attendant delivered the message.

'Acharyavar, sitting here in your presence today, I see myself as a student first and later as male or female. This compelled distance makes me wonder how you impart knowledge with division so distinct in your mind?'

No answer. I paused, felt a quiet rumble, and spoke again. 'As a practising ascetic, one redefines all forms as nameless, discarding the various labels applied to images and forms. Through rigorous practices revered saints like you tear through the many folds of a complex mind. When looking pensively at the moon, it does not flash its name. Distinctions cease, desires ebb, barriers fall, the mind reins in, and an integrated being emerges. I do not understand how my gender poses any threat to your expanded awareness, Acharyavar. Yet, as I am here to learn, I thank you for the privilege. Please accept my gratitude.'

A dull emptiness swept through the doors into the rooms. No one moved but an icy shiver ran down my spine. I sensed a loud silence bursting at the seams and then watched my questions escape through the open windows. I waited in the hope of a refreshing flow of air.

For the next fortnight, I sat for two hours daily at the threshold of the second room, with my back against the wooden door frame, listening intently to Vidyanand muni's elaborate recitation. I received a veiled, sublime conveyance of subtle realms, their inhabitants, and the hidden aim. A new bud arose, and in time, I nourished it with effort.

I was twenty-six. By then, I knew naivety hinders progress. So even though I called out the absurdity, I did not forget my purpose. In time, through the teachings, I learnt the description, invocation, and manifestation of earth-spirit beings. I chanted special mantras that held keys to a sublime elegance. The image and form I mistook for Sri, was Padmavati, a demigod or a Yakshya. I learnt of beings that do not exist in bodies yet reside just above the earth's surface. They attract matter, assisting material aspects of the planet, such as a healthy body, material progression, wealth, and those in search of purposeful recognition.

After the teachings with Vidyanand muni, I stayed silent for many evenings. I had much to absorb. When I lay on my bed, looking at the ceiling, I felt frustrated and sympathetic towards the renunciate. Yet, I am grateful to him as a teacher who taught me far more than I went seeking. I made a few promises to myself: Never submit to divisions created by social power, religious dogma, and control. As much as possible, do as you say and say exactly as you do. The freedom to speak is an allowance we give ourselves. I allow myself to speak without fear and when I am wrong, I bow down. It turns into an opportunity to redefine any redundant thought or idea.

In my daily interactions, I strongly advocate a balance of gender roles for a sustained existence. I believe neither to be lesser. Parallels extend equally. They co-exist, the two being co-dependent . . . interdependent. Every mother must instruct her children of this sublime interdependence.

In the many interactions, I discovered that often, heads of religious organisations walk in a strange manner with their heads mostly bowed in a resigned silence. I often wondered if they raised their eyes to meet themselves in the mirror at night. What do they see when none is looking?

However, I also met a few who walked aloof yet never alone. Sant Nagpal baba also invoked the force of 'Sri'. People revered him as a *siddhatmaa*. I met the founder of a famous temple in Chattarpur, Delhi, in 1989. He addressed each man as Shiv— the performer, and every woman he met as devi—the force behind the one who performs. One is incomplete without the other. Therefore, he too insisted on the equality of parallels.

Nagpal baba dedicated the Chhatarpur temple to a powerful force; a deity that lived in his being—Devi Katyayni. He was a quiet man and addressed me as Devi Kalyani. The last time I met him was after he suffered a fall in the Himalayas. It forced him into a wheelchair. Yet, his eyes shone with the light of a thousand suns, brimming with a child-like enthusiasm.

'Babaji, the likes of me shine in your simplicity and learn. You bless each person who visits you,' I said at one such meeting. While looking at his frail body, I asked in an emotionally charged moment, 'Why can't you heal yourself at this time of agony?'

He smiled and replied, 'Devi, we meet the actions of the body within the body itself. No one can escape the balancing scales of time, matter, and gravity. This applies to all creatures irrespective of their impressions, status, race, colour, accomplishments, and deeds. However, even though the elemental body suffers, the antas (the core) remains untouched.'

That evening I wrote in my diary: 'A body goes through the pain of a predicament. It cannot touch the eternity within. Even in the intensity of Babaji's pain, his eyes exuded the same continuous glow. The brain and the heart have a clear solidity through biological sciences. The mind divides into the intellectual mind and the emotional mind where both are assessed through knowledge and the senses respectively. But the *atman* or the abstract spark of continuity is unseen or hidden. Unknown, it remains a religious ideology at the most.

In my little understanding, the atman is a feeling of intense warmth and a powerful glow within which strikes just like a matchstick in a dark tunnel. A glorious effulgence I saw shining through Babaji's eyes. Like a flame. It dances to its own tune. An abstract continuity—*shashvat;* eternal, impossible to pollute, manipulate, touch, or imprint upon.

Events and situations impress upon the body or the mind—intellectual or emotional bodies. Mantras and siddhis affect the *tattvas* (the manifestations of all consciousness). Nothing impresses upon the atman. How can you impress upon a flame? It is not possible.'

So, how do I know the atman as effulgence? I do not see it, but I have bathed in its glow. I have walked with bare feet on scorching sands, observing, and witnessing the shifting tides of the ocean. As I look behind me, I witness my footsteps making their own history as I tread on.

On a lazy gilded afternoon,
my fragrance
drifts through a pink city
and I, a naïve magnolia
turns even rosier.
On a crisp winter morning,
a sun-kissed girl
peeps in, peeps out
of her bedroom window
and she,
steals away my rosy hue.
In the soft pink of a twilight
when bells chime in a temple,
this world
walks under my silhouette,
and bathes in
my fragrance.

21

Panigraha

While penning my observations in haiku verses, I look out to the sprawling lawns at Panigraha. This venue doubles as my office and a space for events and gatherings. The glass patio doors deliberately slow down the movement between me and the people out in the garden, decorating for a wedding ceremony. Fresh coronets of carmine roses and a thousand strings of marigolds in canary and fiery orange interfere with a creative thought. Distracted, I watch the women animatedly balancing straw baskets on their heads. I follow their tantalising goldfish-coloured ghagras flirting with peacock-hued odhnis. Paradise from a distance.

I sigh and look at my wristwatch. I write the haiku I started, prepare an oratory sequence for the ceremony, and sit through two counselling appointments. At both sessions, I spoke for the first five minutes and then, sipping a cup of chai, listened to clients looking for consolation, validation, and heaps of reassurance. It is now 4 p.m. and there was much to do. I feel as excited as I did the first time when I conducted a traditional Vedic wedding. I am not a pundit (a priest ordained by religious orders). I am a woman equipped with adequate research in ritual and ceremonial knowledge. This information is available for all to access and tonight, in an expectant twilight descending royally in both colour and spectacle, I will perform. Tonight, I will watch myself as convenor of a Vedic wedding ceremony. An elaborate tradition organised at a precise date and time chosen through the Panchangam (Indian almanac). The stars must align for the union.

Most Indian weddings in their jazzy coordination and hyper-illuminated demonstration contradict the distressed chaos on the streets just outside the venues. It is like suddenly entering the threshold of a stimulated world of respite, leaving reality behind. Trampled upon, the sideways lie wretchedly abandoned while loud festivities amplify pretentious proclamations. I insist on the need for revelries; celebrating relationships, communication, and camaraderie, all important for the social human. Yet I cannot ignore the contrast.

It is a deceitful sight, I have to say. I do not look the part. Dressed in the opulence of a Kanjeevaram silk sari complimented with gold and ruby drops, the wayward plain-looking male 'pundit' stands redundant. To the witnessing eye, it is almost a noble stake into the inner circle of a much-guarded profession. It saddens me to observe how a beautiful earthy ceremony centred on sustenance and harmony still begs for the sensitivity of a woman's voice and touch. Yet, tonight was different.

I took my sandals off near the *mandap* and seated myself in the lotus position. Inspecting the rose petals, marigolds, and jasmine flowers for their freshness, I organised them in plates made of banana leaf, drew a specific rangoli pattern with rice, turmeric, and vegetable colours and arranged a coconut traditionally included as a symbol for the *lagan* ceremony—a transcendent union of two beings. Cross-checking all the elements needed, I relaxed, asked for a cup of tea, and mingled with the guests of the bride and groom.

As for the ritual, the pleasure always multiplies if it is a smooth sailing. A ceremony inviting the cosmos to take part deserves appreciation for the past, present, and future of the blessed couple in the asking. I referred to my diary now and again, teasing the bride, instructing the nervous groom, and laughing with his mother, a close friend. I explained the ritual to the witnesses on either side, weaving timeless threads for an interdependent future.

After a deep breath and a pause, looking around, I smiled reassuringly. I am one among them. Human and vulnerable. In that moment, I observe a redefined performance. I felt grace and freedom in each syllable I chanted. Like millions of released particles, the sounds tiptoed into my belly, chest, hands, and spine and then gushed out through my nostrils, mouth, and eyes. As I raised the pitch, I discovered words unfolding not as a language but as bouncing bubbles of serenading rhythms. Millions of tiny implosions surrounded my being within a magnified atmosphere.

Later, I heard comments of how some were distracted, others delighted, and many stunned. I smiled at confused faces struggling to shift and redefine their references and images of a traditional Hindu wedding. One young man in his thirties, Krishnan, commented on how this was his first wedding ritual where he felt involved with another's ceremony.

'I did not know any of this, I have learnt today. Finally, enjoying the beauty and common sense in my own customs, I feel proud of inheriting tradition. No one had ever explained it the way you did. It was not aloof, boring, or vague. Thank you,' Krishnan said.

Listening to him gave me immense strength and hope. Although reduced to the perfect capitalist trap, matrimony in its more elusive sense, facilitates a crucial step for humanity's growth. A fertile ground for commitment, emotional stability, and continuously thriving communities. It is a familial structure that provides for constant learning, sad and joyful curves, and opportunities for the conscious evolution of humans.

Professionally, officiating Vedic weddings remains a thriving business for a privileged caste of men. Why must a profession afford such exclusive power to a minuscule section of the same class of men who force stupid, ignorant, and obsolete restrictions on women? Religion, with its diverse interpretations, has reached a new high where political violations twist and turn concepts into complex anomalies. An extensive patriarchal spread maintains the algorithm, suppressing and repressing populations through advocating stagnated beliefs.

On a recent trip to the most lucrative temple of a revered feminine deity, my eyes searched for change in the 21st century. I longed to see at least one woman in the inner sanctum. None. Rather, she floated like a dead leaf in an atmosphere thick with unwarranted male pride. Many stood in long queues of submission and conformity, gloating at a woman's idol adulated by a man.

Ironically, I did not enter the profession to antagonise a deep-rooted caste hierarchy or patriarchal supremacy. Rather, like thousands of women across the world, I grew to believe in my intelligence and ability to discern intelligibly. It was a natural progression. I simply refuse the undermining disparity, fearmongering, and continued patronising attitudes of so-called keepers of tradition. I know time is short, there is much to do, and I do not waste precious seconds.

It was back in the winter of 1994 when a friend confided that she was in a mature relationship with a younger man. They longed for a wedding, a validity for living together in a reserved community. The families consented, although the nervous mother looked my way for reassurance. Both sides were anxious about the outrage in their communities over a woman's second marriage with a younger man and him marrying a divorced woman. All prejudices concealed in a spiritual, educated, diverse, tolerant, democratic society.

Anyway, after dinner that evening, Lata voiced her wish; she wanted me to perform the rites for their Vedic wedding. I looked at her for a while, and all I saw was her innocent wish for a beautiful union and an opportunity for two people to share their days in togetherness amid a frenzied world. Imagining this perfect picture, I exulted, clapping my hands together and Lata thought I agreed. That was it. The joy on Lata's flushed, tear-streaked face left me with little choice. It felt honourable, and I yielded.

Although I knew the chants, I had never conducted the rituals. In its pristine form, the Vedic ritual of marriage is an invitation to the cosmos as witnesses to a union widely believed as pre-destined in the macrocosm. I was keen on researching each aspect of the ceremony and following it to the tee. So, I spent the next week studying the *Taittriya Upanishad*. It is in the eleventh *anuvaka* of *shiksha valli* that describes the *grihasutras* and the *vivaha samskara*—the ritual of marriage. I prepared the thirty-one notes needed for the ceremonies and checked with experienced associates on the propriety of the ritual. Combining the explanations provided with in-depth knowledge of astrology, chants, and fire rituals, I discovered a soft, dreamy magnificence in each element of the Vedic nuptial process.

On the day of the wedding, I chose an antique cream-coloured Kanjeevaram sari woven with gold paisleys on the *palla*. I matched its extravagance with plain gold leaf earrings that touched my nape and wore fresh mogra flowers in my hair. The vulnerable bride dressed in a rich burgundy sari with gold-bordered silk, and I prepared the mandap meticulously.

I can still smell that memory of Lata's family home in Defence Colony, Delhi. I was twenty-nine then and loved every moment of those joyous smiles and tears. The families on both sides complimented the ceremony. I observed the wedding ritual as a renewed effort to educate myself further.

After this event, I conducted four more wedding ceremonies for clients and friends on personal requests. They were all quiet affairs. In 2009, I steered yet another nuptial for a minister's daughter in Jaipur. It was a lavish affair and I laid explicit instructions—no publicity, no press.

Then, in November 2011, seventeen years after my first brush with this ritual, I convened one more traditional nuptial in Jaipur at the Jai Mahal. I invited a journalist friend who worked with a leading local newspaper. She could not attend on short notice and misunderstanding my personal invite, assumed I was asking for media coverage. Without seeking any clarity, she sent a colleague in her place, informing him I was the 'pundit' for the ceremony. Now this man, seizing the opportunity of a sensational story, informed television journalists. A crew of media personnel ended up at the wedding demanding interviews with me.

The next day press articles and coverage presented the story as a landmark for women. It was great, I thought. But among the readers were some professional male colleagues; people who tolerated my work for all these years, simply because I displayed no tags on my sleeve. They protested the break in tradition with banners, black flags, placards, and a march through the old city of Jaipur from Johri Bazaar to Bapu Bazaar. The community condemned a Sindhi woman for officiating a Vedic ceremony. Local newspapers splashed my name—'Nirmala Sewani, a traitor of tradition, an instigator and a destructive influence on our mothers, daughters, sisters, and wives. A woman dares to walk all the sacred grounds barred for women through the last few centuries.'

Journalists argued each other's opinions on print media for days after the first telecast. They mainly stated the Vedic scriptures prohibit women from conducting any sacred ceremonies. It is necessary to uphold heritage and tradition for future generations and thus it was not only appropriate but urgent to condemn the act. Their vain arguments forced me to call the local newspaper, asking them to print my opinion. Well, I took the bait, and they obliged. I wrote this response: 'I demand evidence to know which scripture states that women cannot perform rites. In fact, I state here from the examples of Gargi; a female rishi from the (Garg Samhita)—a Vedic text which depicts the equal contribution of women in all religious ceremonies.'

Soon after my outburst, I left for Delhi, attending to the usual business of scheduled appointments and work. Every other day, I received calls from my confidante and friend, Mohan, with updates on the ongoing debate. A week later, on a Tuesday morning, as I was preparing to leave for Jaipur, he called again saying the controversy had taken another ugly turn. It had turned political. Women's organisations had come out to counter the protests now. Mohan advised me to remain in Delhi and not make any more statements. It was not an easy phase for anyone, affecting my family and friends too. Conducting marriage ceremonies is not something I speak much about. It is personal, and I have performed about twenty-five wedding rites in all. I just love the ritual and all the splendour for its beauty and grandeur. Anyway, after a fortnight, I was desperate to return. There were fewer protests, but the debate continued. In the meantime, a women's welfare organisation, Shakti Stambh, intervened, taking the case up as an issue for a woman's equal rights. They questioned the validity of an age-old assumption. A representative of the organisation argued that if a woman can be a police officer, an astronaut for NASA, and a prime minister then why can't she be a pundit who solemnises a sacred rite that involves both a man and a woman equally?

Arguments continued back and forth, and two well-intentioned male colleagues, Vinod Shastri and Pramod, tried defusing the tension. I decided it was time to return to Jaipur and called on the head of the *Bhaskar* news agency the day after I arrived. We thought of solutions to this ongoing story. He reasoned behind the controversy, and it revealed the many faces of a politically fuelled agenda. We agreed on three points: First, it was important to defuse the situation. Second, mostly because women were supporting my case, we knew it clearly disturbed the old order. Lastly, we wanted to leave an impression on the men who instigated this protest.

So, using the editor as an alibi, I asked him to convey a message to the protestors. The message read, 'So far, Nirmala Sewani's work revolved around family and clients in Rajasthan and closed circles, but news travels fast and if it reaches the national press, she will definitely benefit from the publicity. Small businesses may well bear the brunt because of her knowledge and capabilities. In view of that, I wonder if it is wise for the local community to continue their agitation or defend Nirmala who backs every word she speaks with actions?' That was it. The protests died in the next week, and since then I have continued officiating weddings for a few more friends and extended family.

Fifteen years later, it is now a trend for women to administer wedding ceremonies. Another seed grew into a nourished tree—a silent resilience with hope for the future.

However, I continually encounter resistance from afar and close quarters. At the recent wedding of my niece, her grandparents protested my wish to perform the wedding rites. Their conditioned minds could not digest change. At another wedding, the family excluded a widowed daughter from the ceremonies, and I refused to proceed till they did not give her a respectful place. The constant rituals of the moon, stars, and planets in the sky do not exclude any corner of the earth. So how can I?

I trudge on with assurance from the many languages of celebration. The purpose is universal—the joy of a union. For this simple reason, marriage is sacrosanct. Yet somewhere in the mind, a conflicting thought pops up, saying, beware, marriage is a hoax, it is a social edifice and an uncertain decision. But does it have to be that way? Instead, what if I focus on a creative process? Then I may savour the exquisite feeling of sharing with another, of gazing into another's eyes, of feeling an intimacy, and of a bonding in matrimony.

I continue the search for promise in the foundation of a union. The ethic of a nuptial evolved over centuries in all its diverse forms to regulate the procreation and sexual desires of the human species. Yet, far more than a need for social structure, marriage fuses communities in a sacred thread of togetherness and love.

Astrologically, a merger happens when there is an alignment or a collision of stars for two beings. A natural, uncomplicated moment. A reciprocal shift transpires in the alliance. Directions change, procreation happens, past impressions iron out, and expansion takes place. I see a sweet, sublime arrangement when one being dances with another in the process of constant expansion.

For me, even though Yogesh Mishra steered my desires at an early age, my father coaxed me into meeting a man two years older than me. In an arranged alliance, my fiancé, Soni, who was a jeweller, became the centre of my world. We courted for a while. His mother and I took to each other like old friends, and she was keen for us to marry, but a month after the engagement, doctors diagnosed a rare cancer in her body. I focused on taking care of Soni's mother and spent long hours at their home.

Ten months later, on a mid-week morning, my father came in early, asking Maa and me to sit in the living room. He looked agitated as he paced the room with his hands behind his back. 'Nirmala, I have broken ties with Soni's family and there will be no mention of them in this house from today,' he said.

Although horrified, I did not ask for explanations. I learnt much later that Soni's father commented on my carefree spirit and unusual ways, while Soni stood there like a passive spectator. He did not express his confidence and trust in me with his father.

'I have not raised a fearless, independent thinker just to tie her to a weak pillar that cannot support her intelligence and strength,' father said to my mother. I knew the finality in his voice. Heartbroken, I travelled to Delhi and stayed with my friend Sunny. Soon afterwards, I heard that Soni's mother died of cancer.

I encountered a strange, vulnerable silence after this episode. It took months to walk out of my burrow, but when I did, I moved forward in contemplation. One strong wind and it takes so much with it. I chose to believe in a life which begins anywhere. Any incident, sad or joyous, enables a dormant seed to rise, bloom, and blossom. I matured, diving deeper into my first love—the combinations of the causal effects, astrology, the planetary positions, and its connection to the emotional body.

Yet that journey of ten months was a precious unfolding. In serving the mother, I learnt to care for another. With my fiancée, I felt an intimacy, a longing for that one person out of a million. A miniature world of my own within the world we inhabit together. Momentarily, I dropped into my heart. Discovering the tenderness of love, its strength, its turmoil, and its weakness, I moved on to witnessing the essence; the synchronous movement in a connection. Walking to the other end of this bridge, I now know the feeling and sense another's pain and anxiety far better than I did from the periphery.

After yearning for a man I had opened myself to, I surrendered. I took the blow, and it cut me up, but a few years later, I chanced upon a picture of this man looking more mature, healthier, and with children by his side. I felt nothing for this changed form and had a realisation: attachments and emotions are a limitation of the body, form, or shape. When I thought of this man, I had a form in mind—a unique face, body, and mind. My body associated the love, pain, and agony with that particular form. But when the form changed, the same body separated from the emotion of it. This is like a mother's attachment to her children. She may love others too but holds a special attachment for her child—a unique form. If she loses her child, she yearns for that form.

I discovered the beauty of the human body. It acts as a vital vehicle, medium, or instrument for harnessing an all-pervading energy. Love and attachment to another form cannot touch the far more expansive light within us—the spirit. Ironically, the body also houses this spirit. So ultimately it acts as a medium for the emotional body, the subconscious, and our connection to the cosmic body.

One night, I felt a colossal pain beyond the causal body. The link, the chain, or the thread connecting all animate and inanimate life and each particle became clear in a whirling sequence. I vibrated, witnessing an infinite interdependency of all life as I felt hurled to an unknown epicentre. I saw the male and female form as two aspects of the one being. Nature is the coalition of these two interrelated, ever-engaging and never-alienated opposite polarities. They exist in opposite directions, yet one does not exist without the other. I vibrated in this whirling. A bitter-sweet pain hard to forget.

I woke with a strong affirmation of co-existence. Life exists on a sacred thread in the merger of male and female aspects in every speck of life. I also realised that friendship is the fragrance of love.

Our intimacy,
does not think
does not know
does not hide
does not show.
It just fulfils us both
in each other.
We are not
complete
or incomplete
we have no wish
or desire,
just fulfilling us both
in each other.
Our intimacy
offers nothing
no frills
no trinkets
no tokens
no display,
just devotion and
reverence
fulfilling a life.
Our intimacy,
disappearing into one another.

22

A Carefree Odhni

The doorbell rang longer than usual on a chilly winter afternoon in the middle of January, way back in 1987. It must have been a public holiday because we were all home. It rang again. Long and urgent. I walked into our modest living room where father sat reading half a dozen newspapers. Soon, Maa walked in with two women beside her, but my gaze quickly shifted to the left. I stood captivated by a beautiful young girl and wondered what attracted me to her. Was it her sharp jawline, her silk scarf or those eyes that refused eye contact?

Maa nudged me before disappearing into the kitchen. I tore my eyes away from the teenager who now sat next to her mother on the two-seater sofa. With a deep breath, I took my place next to Daddy.

The tall woman folded her shaking hands. Daddy and I looked at each other.

'I have heard a lot about you, Nirmala ji, from a cousin who lives here in Jaipur. Please help me. My name is Sujata and I teach math at the government primary school in Kota. This is my daughter, Apsara. She is sixteen. We came here by the early morning bus. It took six hours to get here,' the woman said, placing her right hand on her daughter's knee.

'How can I help?' I asked.

But the woman struggled to speak and choked on the tears she failed to stifle any longer. I ran to the kitchen, returned with water, and waited. Sujata looked at my father and then towards me.

'Last week, after lunch at school, I felt a sharp spasm in my stomach and came home earlier than usual. I saw the bedroom door shut as I walked through the corridor. Unusual, I thought and opened the door to see my husband on top of a thin female figure. I shouted his name. He still wore an unbuttoned white shirt, and his pants were down below his knees. Instinctively, I slammed the door behind me and walked closer. The girl under him was Apsara, our daughter. I screamed like I had never known I could, slapping and kicking his body hard enough to push him away. All while my daughter sat up naked. A hideous secret revealed itself. Apsara scrambled for her clothes and ran out of the room, shaking like a leaf that had suddenly felt the force of a barbaric wind,' Sujata said.

She sobbed again. Too uncomfortable to look at my father, I looked at the young girl named Apsara—a fairy. It is one translation of her name. A celestial maiden trampled upon. I have yet to meet a sharper, more expressive face than hers, but I searched deep into those vacant eyes. I needed to see the remnants of a lost spark, at least for my sanity. I had heard nothing of the kind before. I did not know what to do with it. Yet now I knew why I stood frozen. I saw what I could not comprehend in my perfect world. I had to look away until I heard Sujata speak again.

'I thought it was his first attempt at violating my girl, but no,' Sujata choked again. 'He started assaulting her at fourteen. For two years I watched my daughter shrivel but could not understand why. He threatened her. I was gullible, busy, and too blinded to see it. He beat me many times since then, warning me of the consequences if I made any more noise. When I sobbed asking how he could shame his daughter, he said, "I planted this tree, so why on earth would I not taste its ravishing fruit?"'

I heard newspaper sheets rustle in anger. 'Baby, you must do all you can.' It was my father's trembling voice. Gobsmacked, I looked down at the cemented floor. I was twenty-two years old, studying sociology, and though I had come across a wide spectrum of situations, none felt as repulsive as this one. All the ideas of morality I understood so far, the beliefs I held and every other rational picture I had stored as future reference blew out of my ears with a force I cannot define. My head burst at its seams while I visibly felt my old self fall with a thud. The earth spun too fast, and I called out to Ganesh for help. I closed my eyes for a moment, took a deep breath and a steadier me kicked back into her body.

'You must leave the city immediately. The man will not leave so easily. He will torment you for the next two years,' I said, still uneasy to look at my father.

'But how will I support myself and my daughter? I have nowhere to go. I am staying with my cousin here for two days. I cannot tell anyone, not even my family. If word goes out, Apsara's future will take a far more hopeless turn. No one will believe me,' Sujata said.

'I believe you, but you must believe in yourself. This is not the time to fear. Come back in the morning. Nothing will happen to you or your daughter. Apsara will become a teacher just like you one day.'

Sujata and her daughter had tea with my mother and left. Father stood up and walked straight out of the house. I sat there quietly for the next couple of hours.

That evening, I picked up the phone and called a minister in the state government who I first met as a client. I asked if she could arrange for the urgent transfer of a government teacher from Kota to Jaipur. She assured me of her support but said it might take a month.

The next day, Sujata and her daughter returned, and I told them to move out of the house as soon as she returned to Kota and then contact me. She found a one-room flat far from her home but obviously returned to the same job. The husband continued to torment the two women. Sujata called after ten days, and I heard the panic in her voice. She feared for her daughter's life. So, I told her to apply for medical leave and move to Jaipur. In the meantime, her transfer letters came through.

Once the women were safe in Jaipur, my friend ordered the police to arrest the man. At the court hearings, this man repeated his morbid words. A decade and a half later, Sujata came to meet me once again with a box of cashew nut *burfi*. Apsara was now a lecturer at the university.

I did not work professionally then, but over the years, I have accumulated a thousand stories though never another as revolting as that. I discovered an uncomfortable silence where women remain oblivious to the psychological and cultural gaslighting they endure. Rather, they continue to defend their dependency, normalising every anomaly, while every ounce of their independence stifles in dark corners. Seldom, there are cases where the man falls prey to a scheming woman too. Either way, a death occurs. Integrity perishes. Humanity dies.

I own responsibility when interacting with people. As much as possible, when speaking to a woman, I steer conversations to arouse her intelligence and question the underlying fear she feels. I encourage a man to identify and question the toxic biases ingrained in him as a child because unless men dig deep to excavate their unconscious, cultural prejudices, and re-educate their minds, it is futile to expect change. During consultations, at public platforms and speeches, I ask women to think seriously about financial autonomy, because it holds power. The power to influence, dictate and control.

There are several villages that surround the larger towns of Rajasthan and many of us have extended family in these places. In March 2018, a young forty-five-year-old man in our family died of a prolonged illness, and I travelled to meet the inconsolable mother. It was a warm afternoon, and after the customary condolences, I sat in the veranda with twenty other women from the village, all in attendance around the matriarch.

I watched the younger daughter-in-law; her bony frame wrapped in a flowing ghagra, and her face covered with an odhni that was tied way below her navel. She fidgeted now and again trying to keep the other end of the scarf above her head and finally held it between her teeth. The woman sat close to me. I knew she wanted to say something, but hesitated, looking over to her husband in the far corner of the courtyard. I nudged her on while complimenting the *tulsi* tea she had made.

'Bai sa, it is a difficult situation. I am trying to make ends meet with these two young boys and their father. It has not rained for a long time and our piece of land lies wasted too. I keep thinking of the highway close by. If I could manage a small shop, life may become easier for us.

I nodded while looking at a sad mother-in-law and the peeping husband. Rani's older boy was dragging his worn-out slippers aimlessly in the afternoon heat. She spoke of selling a bit of everything in the little stall to keep her children fed and at school. Trucks and lorries frequented the highway, and she was sure of a decent income. Her husband had little money to spare after his addiction to alcohol.

I looked at the mother-in-law and she agreed it would help. The children could go to the local school if there was enough money to buy books. All the while I heard quiet shifting and murmuring all around. No one interfered, but they all watched intently as Rani's odhni slipped down from her head and I saw her battered cheek and jaw.

My right hand rose sharply in reaction as I pointed to the man in the doorway. I looked straight at the mother and then turned to Rani. 'If this man lifts his hand to hit you again, grab his hand back, and smash it down to break the force.'

Rani spoke through her recovered veil, 'Bai sa, he is physically strong, I am frail. It will do nothing. He will beat me more. It is enough already!'

I softened, 'Yes, I agree but know that when he drowns himself in alcohol, he is weak, he is insecure. Remind yourself of your strength, and the strength of a community that supports each other. Prepare and strike back at his most vulnerable moment. Fear falls quickly when you rise together. So, help each other. Eventually, the beating will have to stop.'

A deep psychological dependency showed its ugly face yet again. Women, in all their different environments, face an endless conflict between survival, self-esteem and maintaining tradition, leading to a complicated web of fears, anxieties and discontent. The repression turns deeper with the turn of each decade. It hovers just above us like a dubious cloud, surfacing now and again to cage those who suggest change, oppose restrictions or wish for more freedom.

Personally, I have seen my sisters, friends, and women clientele struggle through their relationships. Economic independence gave my girls the self-confidence needed to command respect in their environments. A common example of exclusion is when girls and women excuse themselves from rituals because it is that time of the month, of menstrual cycles—a natural process. So, when I visit homes to perform yagyas and notice a female member of the family missing, I always inquire about her absence. Mostly, I put my foot down and ensure their inclusion, but sometimes consequences follow, and girls are too fearful to rebel. However, there is less societal pressure on working-class women, even though a man always exerts his physical prowess one way or the other. Here, both partners contribute equally, and the relationship stabilises to some extent.

I also confront a deeply disturbing, unconscious resignation in women. Many are forced to become what our environments instruct us to believe. Within the applied hereditary conditions, an unconscious expectation arises, and a girl child begins her journey as a lesser being. This callous bias leaves her with no option but to develop in a resigned, toxic silence among family, peers, teachers, and employers. In her naivety, she carries this excess bag wherever she goes, and then passes it down to her kind as an offering. It clings on like ivy, far worse than the shadow, well disguised under falsified sheaths of patience, endurance, sacrifice, and dignity. Poisonous fumes emitting out of a systemic habit are hard to shed. She performs just as her mother did. Occasionally, she revolts, only to be snubbed or hushed by another matriarch. Social stigma imprints a fear way deeper than the marks of a belt on the back. It is a silent killer.

Two literate women from Udaipur—a mother and her daughter—came to me for counselling. The daughter had an abusive, alcoholic husband. When she resisted, he broke her finger. The mother did not raise an alarm or retaliate. She did not support her daughter and somehow thought the miraculous hand of God would help. Her excuse was, 'I do not want the relationship to break because they have a small daughter. That little child will not have two parents to depend on. Also, it will bring such a bad name on our family.'

A bleak repetitive story retold in a single line. A pattern the little girl is bound to follow. The women were teachers at a college. So deeply rooted is this fear of communal boycott that they sacrifice their daughters to it. A sacrifice; the unconscious bias of a mother towards her daughter, of a mother-in-law towards her daughter-in-law, passed down from me to you, from grandmothers to granddaughters, aunts to sisters and nieces to newborn babies. This frustrates me the most. These mothers and grandmothers crave a boy, an heir to the ancestral clan. They flaunt a boy in the sky, encouraging his dominance while they bury their girls in the earth. A drowning reality. And I still hang on, holding my breath, waiting, till I meet a bold, enthusiastic young one with hope brimming through her fearless words. I exhale and live another day. I wish, I anticipate, and I smile.

Tamanna, a dear friend, client, and an upper-middle-class woman, on one casual occasion, celebrated the strong influence I had on her life and wondered out loud, 'I often wish for a swap in our places,' and then added after a deliberate pause, 'In the next lifetime, I want to be you, Nirmala.'

'What makes you say that?' I asked.

'I love your independence. You are so free.'

'What do you mean by independence? Are you less independent, Tamanna?' I asked, shifting my chair slightly to face her directly.

'For me, independence does not mean the freedom to move around. I have that liberty too, but you have the freedom to implement your thoughts,' Tamanna said.

I stared at her, my pen in mid-air, and asked, 'Are you implying you do not have the freedom of thought?'

'I do not allow myself to turn those ideas into a reality and therefore restrict my freedom.'

'Why Tamanna?'

'Because I have children and my family is the priority.'

'Yes, I understand. It is something I hear every day. The invisible chains of family, and children, among various other commitments, turn women into complacent doormats.'

Tamanna shook as I touched a raw nerve. Defence mechanisms kicked in and she hid behind sheets of self-sacrifice; sheets stained with tearing emotions, heavily soiled under the burden of resistance. In the next moment, I watched her torn apart. She broke through her accustomed guard as tears streaked her face. The pent-up, self-demolishing silence of decades came to the surface and, panicking, Tamanna ran out of the room gasping for air.

Half an hour later, in trying to reconcile the chaos a sentence had created, I was far more aware of the larger picture—the predicament of a woman meshed in complex constructs. The pretence or the ignorance of satisfying ethics versus simply indulging the rules laid down for social compliance. Once again, I witnessed the silence of generations that never question the legitimacy of subjective morality.

Tamanna deliberately discarded her thoughts as insignificant and silly, subjecting herself to self-criticism. She self-isolated her wishes to express herself freely while hiding behind a garb of responsibilities. In her role as a mother, wife, and daughter, she controlled and enslaved the creative woman within and believed she had behaved responsibly.

I counselled my sisters during their pregnancies to nurture the baby in the womb with intuition and a reinforced sense of freedom. This is because each human being, irrespective of the vast separations, constantly seeks its identity. A process that begins in the womb. Despite the entangled wires of historical references, this existential search never ceases. Instead, it pushes further like the honeybee that dives to the centre of a flower, disappearing into its bosom. And though this feeling nudges and knocks constantly, the overriding need to comply and control at every step reduces the act of spontaneity. Resentment creeps in and one resigns from the search.

In complete contrast, an independent thinker goes through the same performance without bitterness and continues to nurture one's aspirations, eventually turning them into realities. I encourage my sisters to develop more awareness and discipline their minds as a daily practice. Then our responsibilities turn into a meditation. In the genuine sense of the word, responsibility reflects the ability to respond with compassion towards others. Then, one need not look for being anything more than that.

At times, I struggle to perform in a framework that locks away any possibilities of radical change. People come to me for instant solutions—for the magic wand I do not possess. I face a relentless battle; each day I prepare myself to view all forms of life through a universality I refuse to let go of. I reject the division of human beings under the pretext of popular 'categories.' Schisms and distinctions among creatures, human and otherwise, are limited to their physical or mental capacities. I use a common approach; soft, positive, yet bold and forthright so one may walk out with renewed devotion to none other than the self.

Personally, I choose to explore femininity and masculinity as two faces of the same coin. All human beings and creatures have masculine and feminine attributes, irrespective of obvious distinctions. Re-imagining the structure of identity becomes crucial to understanding the delicate balance between the male and female aspects. Their co-existence is vital for sustenance. There is no greater or lesser; rather an equal importance of form (male) and energy (female) in the process of procreation. Ideally, the union of two aspects should complement each other, and occasionally, it does. But humanity functions less from an active, individually responsible position and more from a passive collective—a historical pattern.

And if co-existence is so vital, then why and how does it limit either gender in any way? For instance, 'mothering', a natural phenomenon higher and far beyond any profession created by a human, requires no profitable degree. Just mother's instinct; a precious intimate knowledge almost unknown to the male species. The man observed this phenomenon centuries ago, discovering its limitations. Since then, masculinity pushed ahead playing constant games on the sensitivity of that mother and her womb.

In her immense vulnerability, a woman continuously believes in a dream—of the male species as her protector. A knight in shining armour. He plays the role of a provider and a shield to perfection, while she nurses the baby and its father. Thus, through centuries of historic dominance arose a systemic, irreversible pandemic of physical male power. A chronic disease that feeds off ignorance and thrives through brainwashing. The gullible woman repeatedly falls for the false notion that the physicality of a man nurtures her needs. In time, her dreams shatter, and she craves for an independent thought.

So, I often ask . . . What revised version might define a woman? The question turns into a personal meditation.

A girl with independent thoughts and ideas makes for a grown woman. She believes in nothing but her inherent strength; an awareness that stems naturally, not from a law laid down by patriarchy. This female form comprises a 'complete constitution.' Her capacities arise from the rounded precincts of her womb. There are no sharp edges. The endurance she discovers within these walls creates a male. This male—a man—inherits the extent of his potency, his muscle, his intelligence, and his physicality from her.

A woman in her entirety exudes a wholeness—a totality. This is because she births another whole form, losing nothing of herself in the process. Furthermore, if she chooses not to conceive, she still holds that intrinsic energy available to a woman. If she has not birthed yet, she senses her capacity to in the near future. This creative potential, although personal, expands into the universal. It secures the known with the unknown universes.

'Om poornamadah poornamidam poornat poornamudachyate Poornasya poornamaadaaya poornamevava shishyate.' This Sanskrit shloka captures the essence of a mother with utmost precision. A complicated translation, it essentially means: 'A form that is whole is complete; it is infinite. Infinity plus infinity is infinity, and infinity minus infinity is infinity. In division and multiplication, it is infinite. What is whole remains whole when subtracted or added by itself. Perfection. That is who a mother is.'

In essence, a woman births from her womb a whole new life and remains whole, emerging with a new identity as a mother. She is reborn. So, where does that place her?

Infinite, strong, precise, and free. That defines a woman. She protects, nourishes, and shields too. On the other hand, a man is never reborn as a father. This new position or title adds on as another label to the growing list. Yes, he cares and hurts too while largely accommodating another being in his life—one more to protect. The mounting shield of protection envelops his self, and he swells in it. In his moment of glory, he protects another man too. One of a kind, yet so separated from the sustenance of a mother; a river that nourishes wherever she flows.

So, I refuse to believe a woman was ever inadequate. How could she be? And I dare to evaluate her quality of perfection just a step further. Monitor a woman as she goes about her day. When she stumbles upon imperfection, it agitates her. She sets about putting things in place. Her instincts force a kind of order in a chaotic world. She organises and restores, as she moves through the day. Ironically, a woman's limitations originate from her personality too. As she strives for constant perfection, she constantly drops from her own perfect essence. It creates a permanent fissure, a separation. Complete versus incomplete, perfect versus flawed, good versus bad, right versus wrong, likes versus dislikes, and so on. Judgements spew out in all directions. In fact, the rift reaches such a height of imperfection that it poisons the mind and jealousy sets in. She manipulates for her own security and mostly does not support another woman.

Historically, you will find a man most likely to support another man, but a woman will have self-vindicated reservations about doing the same for another woman. In the want, the desire, and the longing for her male protector, she fails her own kind. This becomes her downfall, and an all-consuming insecure thought arises. It is a condition many women face however progressive their environments may be.

When we do not question but blindly follow the stories our cultures and immediate environments feed us, they bleed into our nervous, digestive, and respiratory systems, clogging the pipes and holding us back. We stop chasing a creative thought, losing sight of the proposed opportunities, and fall into a deep sleep, fitting into the matrix, suffocating, until imagination dies an unnatural death.

So, the casting die may revise and shift a little, but actual change demands the ouster of outdated narratives. Every young girl, a woman, a mother, a daughter, and a granddaughter must re-invent all she knows, believe in what she feels, and intuitively teach a new lesson of equality and respect to the child she births. A young boy, a father, a son, and a grandson may then spread this renewed narrative where an equal co-existence is not only possible but a sustainable reality.

Whichever way one looks at it, as humans we grow and expand through another. When I meet a woman, I use all the tools available to assist her growth. A woman lacks nothing. Before a woman leaves my space, I try to show her—her own magnificence within the magnitude of this beautiful earth.

Shankar laughs when I excitedly raise my voice in exasperation, 'Nirmala di, calm down! Your words fall like drumbeats on a *guangu* (a Mongolian war drum), cracking wildly upon a tough leather hide.'

I ask, 'But who is listening here?'

Well, my ears listen to the words I speak. My thoughts vibrate in ripples to meet their destination in the hearts, minds, and spirits of those waiting at the threshold of their unfolding stories.

Do you feel the same too?
Yes, I remain silent
yet, I have a lot to say.
Why can't I break this silence?
Why can't I throw open
the closed cages of my mind?
What defines this unknown fear
of losing both the personal
and the impersonal?
Why are the wings of my words trapped
within the corrals of my mind?

I want to free these birds
so,
I can live in open spaces.
I remain silent
but yes
I have a lot to say.

23

An Honourable Passing

When I gently touched my father's hand, it felt warm, and his face shone as usual.

'Naani, I think he's alive. He looks so normal. How can you tell he is dead?'

Naani nudged me and said rather plainly, 'Your father is not in this body anymore. If you touch his feet, you will feel death.' I did. His soles felt oddly cold.

This was the first time I looked at death in the eye. Peculiarly calm, no violence, no pain, and it did not frighten me. Daddy passed away in January 1999 when I was thirty-three years old. I foretold his death to a precise date as I had done for many others. It was never as hard-hitting and difficult. I came face to face with a reality I spoke of so accurately but never witnessed. Never had I been in the same room with a dead person.

Stepping forward with a mixed bag of caution, fear, and uncertainty, I blanked out. No tears. It did not sink in because Daddy did not look any different from how he always slept—peacefully. I felt nervous with a tingling sensation I could not shake off. Something went missing in the air around me. Was that an unknown fear of looking at a dead person face to face? Could I feel the trepidation of a new dawn? Or did I suddenly realise the stillness of time? Honestly, I could not tell.

Even though I had predicted my father's death for that day in January and my ears heard he had died, I struggled. Perhaps because I loved him and the physical aspect of death or of destruction lay invisible at that point. It was also because of the precision of my prediction. It is a complex feeling. I feel separated from the others who cannot know yet the same evidence also connects me deeper to a powerful life force running through every particle in the known universe. I cannot escape. An existential interdependency reveals itself. A humbling acceptance envelops me, and I chant within.

My father was good at reading astrological charts and knew the date of his passing too. The 28th of January. He had calculated the time of his death in his diary—18:45 p.m. A spiritual, intellectually aware human being, he had a keen sense of knowing. It is interesting that I did not know his time of passing yet he did. Scheduled for a postoperative eye check-up, Daddy left the house for an appointment that day. My brother-in-law, Jai, sat with him in the car while Shankar drove. They said that as the car passed Birla Mandir, Daddy took an abrupt breath at 18:45 and uttered the words 'Hey Ram.' Life exited through his wide-open mouth, and he collapsed on Jai's shoulder.

The sounds of that evening lie deep in my bones. Footsteps, sniffles, commotion, and an unfamiliar silence. The birds sang a different song, like they were moving to a new house for the night. Sitting on the rug in the far corner of the room, I placed the Gita on a wooden, hand-carved book stand and read the entire scripture from start to finish; all eighteen chapters one by one. I sat still for a long time. In every passing second, I felt something die and something take birth. I fell into a deep silence that night.

Daddy did not call my name in the morning. For the last thirty-odd years, I heard my father when I woke but not on the 29th of January 1999. I witnessed death. It left me feeling older and unusually responsible. A new knowing dawned on me, unveiling the two mysteries—life and death. And certainly, death is the greater mystery. Life takes its time, spreading over fifty, sixty, or eighty years in the happening, but death happens in a singular moment. Intense, often passionate, but in one crowning moment. A climax. A surprise. Death remains a certainty, whereas everything before this moment holds possibilities.

A cycle persists. Life eventually witnesses an end, a separation or death. Time and again. A plant dies, an animal dies, and a human dies. An idea dies, and a relationship dies. It is irreversible, yet regenerative. The morning after Daddy died, I accepted death. I did not cry at all. For a fortnight, I felt my father watching me closely. I felt his impressions, his words, and his presence around me. I still feel the same.

But I also felt light. I felt him as an imprint on this earth, something that existed in the past and still exists in the future. I wrote my thoughts: 'Energy reshuffles and matter goes through a cycle of renewal. Destruction of the elemental body leads to regeneration. When energy collides with matter, it takes a form—a body, a medium. Birth takes place. When the medium perishes, 'pran (life force) rearranges itself. It either goes back to its source or finds another form.

To truly witness a passing, one must shed ideas, concepts, the separation, and the fear attached to the word 'death.' One must empty the references. To die consciously, one must choose to live in awareness. I know the existence of those conscious beings who accept death as an opportunity; they crave the fragrances it offers and anticipate the expanse it seeks. Thus, they live fully, in awe of the next breath. For them, death narrates a different story, a symbolic preparation rather than a fearful demon. Santhara is one such technique for internal cleansing. Practised by a Jaina sect, the logic lies in lighting another candle when the first caves in. A delicate, vulnerable process of cleansing layers in an elemental body; the intellectual body, the emotional body, the blissful body, and the desiring body, all for the crystal-like clarity of the life force within. So, it may pass honourably to the next home and another flame may be lit.

It is like renting a new house, making it a safe home for fifty-odd years, but eventually, the time comes to move, or to vacate. Courtesy demands one leaves this house, at least twice as clean as when first entered. Santhara applies the same lifelong practice in the purified movement of the energy within.

My references to the word purity solely compare to that of a newborn whose body is devoid of habitual programmes. It observes its surroundings in awe of this creation. It does not blink too often. It does not need to. A new arrival witnesses from a distance. Pure and unattached.

With sheer diligence to retrace this purity, people in Jain communities observe various practices in anticipation of a separation. They live each day with the awareness of death. The freedom of an honourable passing is not the prerogative of monks and ascetics but of those who own responsibility for their moments and walk with as much dignity as is possible, given the predicament they live with. A choice pleated into daily existence. But how, you might ask?

In method, men and women eat frugally, relying on mostly liquids. They lead disciplined lives but essentially walk in awareness of the breath, keeping it in the forefront constantly. Not on the back burner. When life ceases, or when the body fails, life force exits from any one vent—the eyes, the nostrils, the ears, or the anus. I have read of three rare exits too—navel, mouth, and an opening above the skull. Name it what you wish, but this life force, this spark of light, exits from one of these windows.

I was nearing forty when I started following the journey of some women in diverse communities across India. I observed the simplicity of their days, their nature of be-ing rather than a constant want of becoming. Cautious of their moments, their actions, and their speech, they were as alive as the rivers, nurturing effortlessly as they moved. *Saral* (simple). *Jo saral hai who hi sahaj hai* (only that which is simple is natural). When the time came, one of them passed through her eyes with a flash of bright light permeating the room. The one who passed through the nose left with a fragrance that lingered for as long as one could hold it. When *pran* (life force) passed through another's ears, I heard a faint but profound hum touching my core. Years later, I felt blessed to witness this great mystery with my mother's passing. These women embraced life in all its colours and eventually the unknown embraced them.

When I turned fifty-five, I suddenly felt Dr Yogesh Mishra's presence and realised he was nearing a hundred years in age. I felt his heights in the folds of the Himalayan mountains, living in a world where myth exists. In the next moment, I knew he would not re-birth. He will live till his karmic bonds with this planet reconcile and the scales tip no more, after which nothing will hold him here. He will not return. Perhaps I will pass, and he will remain.

Death transcends time yet, because this phenomenon occurs in a moment, one fears it. One does not accept that moment, that certainty. Instead, one clings to life. Death comes every day. In each passing moment, something dies. A moment becomes irreversible. In gathering all those moments lived so far, soon one feels the burden. It drains the mind, the body, and a beating heart. Fearful and tired, one cannot dance. The flute plays, but one cannot hear. A baby births and a bud blossoms, but one cannot see. The river flows, yet one stagnates. Though night awaits in an unknown darkness, one expects another breath and yet another dawn. And I reiterate . . . although we live in one world, each one's world is different.

Inundated with a wide spectrum of situations as early as thirteen, I realised the uniqueness of each predicament. This dominates one's thought. Billions of thoughts and a billion worlds. I walk in and out of these worlds, watching, listening, sharing, and conveying, yet ultimately retreating to my thoughts and my world. Gradually, I learnt to observe events and situations from a distance. I became uninvolved. Much like watching a movie. A *drashta* (a witness). Engaged yet detached. Since my mother died, I feel more surrender and dedication in my moments. I have retreated. Solitude is a graceful invitation, an event, a celebration, and an opportunity to feel. I have come to a realisation: *Apne nartan aap hi hain antas mein*—when centred in yourself, you dance to your very own unique tune.

I feel every particle vibrating and gathering momentum towards a collective evolution; an effortless yet powerful life force flowing through the inhale and exhale. When I listen, I hear a profound sound. An echo. A whisper. A heartbeat. I hear all of life in constant meditation. I listen for a long time. I experience it. Shashvat—eternal it is. A continuous movement, in focus and in a deep introspection. In a silent dance.

I stubbornly meditate on this profound silence. A maun, a silence that has filled me. I do not hear the noise anymore.

Your presence,
gives me peace.
When you are there
I can sleep
and dream too.

I always just wait …
for you,
for sleep
and
for peace.
I sense your fragrance
on my body
the moment
I open my eyes in the morning.
Did you caress me all night in my dreams?
Perhaps.

Author's Afternote

After two months of endlessly shuffling through Nirmala's memories, and exploring the nuances of language, we sat in the cool marbled courtyards of the majestic Amer fort in Jaipur. A fairly large, square patio bordered with elegant tall pillars emanated a deep but obscure sense of ancient dignity. Carefully overlapping straw blinds shielded us from the dazzling world. But the glaring eye of a stark desert bounced through the few loose strands of straw, revealing what we hide or escape from. Just like Nirmala's story, I thought and smiled.

We looked across the courtyard, where a few people gathered in the far-right corner of the intricately enamelled marbled floor. An aged, bearded man suspended two awkwardly shaped marionettes from their strings, manoeuvring them with deft strokes. One puppeteer mimicked the characters while another sounded the drum like the receding echo of tide and time. We witnessed the continuity of tradition hypnotising its participants with a few strings pushed and pulled in an almost perfect sequence. All through a folk tale. Nothing went amiss.

After all the time spent with Nirmala, perhaps I found a key. I do not know. My search has just begun.

With gratitude
Annie Miller

Acknowledgements

To the primordial feminine
Thank you . . . for your generosity

Thank you to Sonali Pawar at Hay House India, for her confidence in this project. Thank you to Aditya Jarial for his editorial efforts, honest approach, and immense patience. Thank you to the design team for their enduring cooperation. Thank you to Nirmala's family for their undying support. Thank you to Mr Miller for the steady care. Thank you to our children for constantly pushing us to think differently. Thank you to our friends . . . you are the brightest stars on dark nights.

Shukriya to all for showing us the way.

About Nirmala Sewani

A Master of Psychology, Sociology, and Metaphysical Studies, Dr Nirmala Sewani also recently earned an honorary doctorate for advanced research in the occult sciences and Indian astrology. Conferred the Bharat Nirman award twice, among several other accolades, she has also made valuable contributions towards the preservation of traditional Indian philosophy focusing mainly on the intricacies of Yajur Veda. A major contributor to case studies (1995-2005) in the research on schizophrenia, genetics, and analytical psychology, Nirmala's experience, knowledge, and wisdom stem from a deep-rooted passion for the collective progression of humanity. She has counselled and guided people for over four decades and her uncanny ability to access the subtle worlds continues to attract many more. For Nirmala, magic lies in the voice of a person. She listens intently to reveal what lies behind the spoken word—thoughts, emotions, intentions, and the soul's blueprint.

Nirmala lives a busy life in Jaipur, surrounded by family and friends, yet in her quiet moments, she pens her deepest reflections through her favourite form in poetry, the haiku.

For more information, visit: www.nnirmalasewani.com

About Annie Miller

An artist, editor, translator and a mother, Annie Miller, is also a student of philosophy and myth. Born in England, she now lives with her husband by the sea in south Ayrshire, Scotland. When she is not writing, Annie loves hiking through the many trails of the Scottish Highlands or stippling for hours, creating pictures and portraits with a fine ink pen. *Maun*, her debut book writing project, is a natural extension of her passion for biographies, storytelling, and sharing diverse narratives.

www.anniemiller.co.uk

Glossary

Aahat: External sounds or noise

Aakaar: Shape

Aakash: Atmosphere or sky

Acharya: Teacher, spiritual head, or professor

Agarbatti: Hand rolled incense sticks

Agyaat: The unknown

Agyaya: The mysterious unknowable

Ajmer Sharif: Moinuddin Chishti's shrine with his grave

Alstonia Boonei: A very large, deciduous, tropical-forest tree

Anahat: Internal sound, unstruck sound, or noiseless sound

Antas: Core seat of feeling, faculty of reasoning and clarity, or fundamental core

Anu: An atom or molecule

Anubhav: A feeling or sense

Anuvrat: A Jain movement seeking a non-violent socio-political community of self-transformed people

Aradhika: A female devotee with love as the focus

Asakt: Strong or undefeatable

Ashram: A hermitage, monastic community, or other place of religious retreat

Asura: A demonic being or tendency

Atman: A Vedic spiritual concept, denoting a spark of energy (that exists within all creatures). An atman essentially being a flicker of the totality—the param atman or cosmic fire.

Aum Gam Ganpataye Namah: A mantra enabling the manifestation of a Jupiterean energy or intellect

Aurat Jaat: Woman kind or female species

Aushadhi: Medicines or healing roots, herbs, fruits, and spices

Avastha: State, aspect, stage, degree, or facets

Bagru: A town in Rajasthan

Bai Sa: A term of respect and endearment commonly used for a senior woman

Barkha: A Hindi name for a woman meaning rainfall

Bhai: Brother

Bhen: Sister

Bindu: Dot

Birla Mandir: A temple in Jaipur

Brahmin: An upper caste within Hindu society

Burfi: Indian sweet cakes made with milk and nuts

Chai: Tea

Champa: Frangipani

Chana: Chickpeas

Glossary

Chandan: Sandalwood

Chand-Mund: Chand means body and mund means mind

Chawal: Rice

Cholapattak: A lower garment worn by men, covering the waist downwards to the shins

Dahi: Yogurt

Dasheri Aam: A sweet and fragrant variety of mango

Deepa: A Hindi name for a woman meaning light or a flame

Devas: Divine being or compassionate tendencies

Devi Kalyani: The presiding feminine deity of well-being

Devi: Feminine energy

Devimahatmaya: A philosophical text describing the primordial womb/feminine creation of the universe

Dhoomralochan: Influences of the external/smokescreens

Dhoop: A thick, hand rolled incense made with various herbs, resin, and clarified butter

Dhurrie: A thick, flat woven rug

Digambar: The Sanskrit word Digambara means 'sky-clad', referring to their traditional monastic practice of neither possessing nor wearing any clothes and it is one of the two major schools of Jainism

Diksha: A religious ceremony for monkhood

Diya: Earthen lamp containing oil and a cotton wick

Ganesh: An Indian deity depicted with a human lower body and the upper torso of an elephant

Ganga: The river Ganges

Garbh Pratishthan: A ceremonial process involving the re-establishment of the womb

Gargi: Mentioned in the Grihya Sutras of Asvalayana, she is honoured as a great Indian sage, natural philosopher, and renowned expounder of the Vedas

Gayatri: Universal awareness

Ghee: Clarified butter

Gita: The Bhagavad Gita, often referred to as the Gita, is a Hindu scripture, which is part of the epic Mahabharata

Gokhru: Puncture vine

Grehan: A dark area or shape formed by the obstruction of light when an object comes between the rays of light and a surface

Guggal: Indian bdellium-tree

Gulkand: Crushed rose petals used to make rose jam along with sugar syrup

Guru: A personal religious teacher and spiritual guide in Hinduism who passes his own skill to a student or disciple

Gurudwara: A place of worship for Sikhs

Gyaat: Knowing, vision, or insight

Gyan: Knowing through experiential knowledge, filtered wisdom, and understanding

Halwa: A sweet semolina dessert

Harshringhar: Night jasmine

Havan Kund: A clay or copper pot used for Hindu fire rituals

Haveli: A traditional townhouse, mansion, or manor house

Hukum (Sir): A polite and respectful form of addressing someone

Jaap: Repetition of mantras on a 108 seeded mala

Jai Mahal: A palace in Jaipur that has been converted to a hotel

Jaina: A practitioner or adherent of Jain principles and teachings

Jaiphul: Nutmeg

Jati: A Sanskrit term derived from 'Jatā,' referring to one's origin at birth, often associated with lineage and hierarchical grouping in caste systems

Jau: Barley

Javitri: Mace

Ji: A suffix added to a name as a mark of respect, typically used when addressing an elder or someone in a senior position

Jyotish: The science of tracking movements of astronomical bodies

Kali: A major Hindu goddess with immense power

Kanjeevaram: Handwoven silk and zari embroidery saris made in Tamil Nadu, India

Karmic: Theory of action and consequence

Katha: Folklore rich with ancient wisdom and parables

Kesar: Saffron

Ketu: Imaginary incision point where the moon, while moving from the north to the south, crosses the path of the sun in the zodiac

Khas: Poppy seed

Kleem: Seed of attraction

Kota Zari: Hand spun/woven saris made in Kota, Rajasthan

Kshatriya: The warrior caste

Kumbhak: Steady or concentrated

Kund: Iron or clay vessel for burning fire

Kundli: An Indian birth chart illustrating the positions and influences of planets at the time of birth, specifying their effects in degrees

Lagan: A union or meeting of two individuals

Laghu Parashari: A Sanskrit treatise exploring the predictive dimensions of Indian astrology

Lakshmi: A feminine energy symbolising prosperity and wealth

Lau: Flame, spark of light, or sustenance

Lopa Mudra: An ancient female philosopher from 6th or 7th century BCE

Maa/Ma: Mother

Maanavjati: The classification of a creature as human

Madhukaitambh: Attribute of complacency and laziness

Maha Mritunjaya: Transcendental form

Mahapragya: Qualitative epithet for a highly knowledgeable monk

Mahayagya: The constant movement of the universe

Mahishasur: Attribute inducing fear and doubt/phobias

Maitriya: Advaita philosopher from the 8th century BCE

Makaar: Abrupt exhale

Mala: A string of 108 seeds

Manas: The thinking mind

Mandap: An elevated square decking with pillars on four sides, symbolic of the four directions and a central fire (used for a Hindu wedding ceremony)

Mansagari: Descriptive Sanskrit thesis on Indian astrology authored by the astrologer Janardan Harji

Mantragya: A person proficient in the knowledge and application of mantras

Mantras: Short, coded Sanskrit phrases for specific purposes

Masi: A term of endearment for mother's sister, meaning 'like a mother'

Maun: Dedicated periods of silence

Mogra: Arabian jasmine

Moksha: Freedom from the individualistic approach or 'I'-ness, signifying liberation from self-centered perspectives

Muhpatti: A square piece of white cloth, secured with strings behind the ears, covering the mouth area

Muni: Jain renunciate monks

Naad Yog: The union of internal and external sound or the union between a being and the universe through sound

Naad: The cosmic/atmospheric vibration that surrounds us

Namaskaar: A culturally rooted expression in South Asia, symbolising gratitude and reverence towards the individual being acknowledged

Nani: Maternal grandmother

Navaakar: A Jaina seed mantra for complete protection

Nirvana: Surpassing the cycles of birth and death or freedom from the wavering mind

Odhni: A long drape/scarf tucked over a blouse and skirt in the traditional Rajasthani attire

Padmavati Sasandevi Yakshini: The protective feminine spirit in Jaina mythology

Panchangam (Hindu Calendar): Literally translating to 'five limbs,' it refers to an ancient Vedic almanac featuring tabulations that intricately outline the positions of the sun, moon, and other celestial bodies for both astronomical and astrological purposes

Pangarini: A thin white upper garment worn by Svetambari monks to cover the shoulders and chest like a shawl

Panigraha: Marriage/Accepting one's hand (as offered in marriage)

Parampara: Embedded traditions and enduring practices that are passed down generations

Parijatham: Night jasmine flowers

Paushaak: Traditional Rajasthani dress with a flowing skirt, blouse, and scarf

Poori: Deep fried flatbread

Prabhavvriddhi: To impress upon

Preksha: Complete self-awareness

Pret Vidya: Study of the paranormal or dead

Purak: Ascending

Rahu: Imaginary incision point where the moon, while moving from the south to the north, crosses the path of the sun in the zodiac

Rajnigandha: Mexican tuberose

Raktbeej: A singular drop of blood symbolising a seed that sprouts from the soil

Ram Navami: A Hindu festival that celebrates the birth of Rama on the ninth day of the spring season

Rechak: Descending

Sadhika: A female seeker with knowledge as the focus

Sago: Tapioca

Samadhi: Constant awareness to steady a wavering mind

Samyak Darshan: Authentic perception, deep understanding, or insight

Santhara: A lengthy and consistent discipline aimed at preserving the purity of the human body, which serves as a vessel for light and facilitates its transfer to another body with the same purity

Sardar: A title used before the name of the leader of a tribe or Sikh men who wear a turban

Sari: Indian dress made of a six-metre drape of fabric

Saroj: A Hindi name for a woman meaning a beautiful sunrise

Sattvic Yug: Eon or epoch

Shaastras: A Sanskrit term referring to ancient texts encompassing first principles, philosophy, and ideology

Shashvat: Continuous, uninterrupted, constant, or eternal

Shetavri: Asparagus racemosus

Shri: An honorific title that goes before a name

Shudhi: Purification

Shumb Nishumb: Demonic attributes such as pride and arrogance

Siddhatmaa: A being firmly rooted in the awareness of its expansive nature

Siddhi: Insight, spiritual proficiency, or occult accomplishments

Siddhita: Realisation or established knowing

Sikh: A community of people who follow Sikhism

Sindhi: Socio-ethnic community of people originating from the Sindh region of the old Indian subcontinent (now Pakistan) (Also a dialect spoken in the Sind province in Pakistan and the Sindhi community globally)

Sri: The nourishing aspect of energy

Stupas: The outward appearance

Sufi Dargah: A mystic's shrine built over a grave

Sugandha: A Hindi name for a woman meaning fragrance

Svetambari: (svet means pure or white and ambari means hue or atmosphere) It denotes a sect of Jaina community who wear thin white unstitched garments as a covering

Swar: A Sanskrit term referring to the sound of a musical note corresponding to its name, a vowel, and the breath

Swayam Siddha: The ability to access inner self-knowledge and conscious thoughts

Tagar: Rhizome herb

Taajik Neelkanthi: An academic fusion of Vedic and Arabic concepts within the realm of astrological study and interpretation

Takht: A commonly used wooden bed in Asia, resembling more of a bench with planks designed for sitting

Tantra: The end product, the result, or the expansion of

Tattvas: In the Samkhya school of philosophy, the twenty-four tangible manifestations of creation.

The Great Banyan: A 250-year-old tree in Kolkata, India, covering five acres of land

Tulsi: Indian basil

Ukaar: Inhale

Upanishad: Late Vedic and post-Vedic Sanskrit texts

Vaasantik: Something that begins at the onset of spring

Vada: Spicy fried balls of soaked tapioca

Vaisakh Poornima: Vaisakh is the second month in the Hindu calendar, and Poornima refers to the full moon. This day is also celebrated as Buddha Jayanti, marking the enlightenment of Buddha.

Vashikaran: An instrument that attracts or an attractive force

Vastu Vidya: The ancient Indian science of integrating nature with architecture through symmetry and directional alignment

Vedis: Small, tabled platforms for 4-6 people used for performing fire rituals

Vistaarit: The expansion of a concept, idea, or mantra.

Vivaha Samskara: The ritual of marriage

Yagya: A continuous cosmic ceremony or an individual or communal fire ceremony

Yajur Ved: A Sanskrit Vedic text that delves into rituals and practices

Yaksha Vidya: Occult practices to access beings of other realms

Yantra: An instrument or the vehicle

Yog: Union

Yuvacharya: The designated successor to his guru, serving as the supreme head

www.ingramcontent.com/pod-product-compliance
Lightning Source LLC
LaVergne TN
LVHW040136080526
838202LV00042B/2925